ERRATA – DIVING INSTRUCTION

P. 115. Paragraph 1. Under Men's Highboard Conditions amend as follows:
The competition conditions shall consist of four voluntary dives, the total degree of difficulty of which shall not exceed 7.5, and six voluntary dives without any limit.

P. 147. Line 23. Amend percentages for Bronze Award to 40 per cent, Silver to 45 per cent.

P. 48. (Sections 4 and 5). Addresses should be amended to: Amateur Swimming Association, Harold Fern House, Derby Square, Loughborough, LE11 0AL, Leicestershire.

DIVING INSTRUCTION

DIVING INSTRUCTION

by

N. W. SARSFIELD, M. C.

in collaboration with

The Amateur Swimming Association

Diving Committee

Published Officially for

The A.S.A. by

EDUCATIONAL PRODUCTIONS LTD.

WAKEFIELD, YORKS.

First Published 1953

Revised edition 1957

Revised edition 1960

New edition 1966

Revised 1969

by Educational Productions Ltd.

17, *Denbigh Street,*

*London, S.W.*1

Stores Department: Bradford Road, East Ardsley, Wakefield, Yorks.

Printed and bound in Great Britain by
TERRY AND NEPHEW LTD., WESLEY STREET, DEWSBURY, YORKS.

FOREWORD

Since the first appearance of '*Diving Instruction*', it has become an essential medium through which the teaching of diving has been disseminated and as a result has been sought after by teachers and coaches everywhere.

Facilities for diving are all too frequently sub-standard, particularly outside the big population areas. With his wide practical experience of the sport under all conditions, Mr. Sarsfield has always endeavoured to cater for the teacher operating in these circumstances as well as the more fortunate who have up-to-date equipment and adequate water depth available.

Diving is an extremely progressive sport and new techniques are constantly being evolved. For this reason the author has correctly decided to keep '*Diving Instruction*' in the premier position that it occupies in its field. This has been most admirably accomplished and I am certain that new and old readers alike will find in this revised edition everything they require for the teaching of our chosen sport — Diving.

Jimmie Scott,

C. J. Scott, *formerly Hon. Sec.*
A.S.A. Diving Committee.

CONTENTS

Page

TEACHING, COACHING AND CLASS MANAGEMENT   13

STARTING TO DIVE   35

THE SPRINGBOARD   48

HIGH BOARD DIVING   61

KEY DIVES   82

THE MECHANICS OF DIVING   99

DIVING PROGRESSION   109

ESSENTIAL FEATURES AND THE JUDGING OF DIVING   119

EXERCISES FOR DIVERS   127

THE MEDICAL ASPECT OF DIVING   141

APPENDIX.   146

LIST OF ILLUSTRATIONS

Page

HAND SIGNALS	20
PUSH AND GLIDE	36
THE SITTING DIVE	37
THE CROUCH DIVE	38
THE LUNGE DIVE	39
THE PLAIN HEADER	41
STANDING SPRINGBOARD TAKE-OFF	52-53
RUNNING SPRINGBOARD TAKE-OFF	58-59
RUNNING SPRINGBOARD TAKE-OFF	65
BACK SPRINGBOARD TAKE-OFF	66
FORWARD DIVE PIKED	67
FORWARD DIVE WITH TUCK	68
REVERSE DIVE PIKED	68
BACK DIVE PIKED	70
INWARD DIVE PIKED	71
FORWARD DIVE ONE TWIST STRAIGHT	72-73
FIRMBOARD RUNNING TAKE-OFF	74
FIRMBOARD BACK TAKE-OFF	75
ARMSTAND SOMERSAULT PIKED	76-77
ARMSTAND FORWARD CUT THROUGH WITH TUCK	78
TRANSFER MOMENTUM IN TWIST DIVES	79
FORWARD DIVE STRAIGHT	80
THE PLAIN JUMP FORWARD	83
THE TUCK JUMP	84

A*

LIST OF ILLUSTRATIONS

					Page
FORWARD DIVE WITH TUCK	..	..	..	..	87
FORWARD DIVE PIKED	..	..	..	..	88
INWARD DIVE PIKED	..	..	..	..	93
ANGLE OF TAKE-OFF	..	..	..	..	101

Exercises

	Page
WARMING UP — NECK AND HEAD, ARM AND SHOULDER — PIKE ..	129
TUCK, TWIST, BALANCE	129
STRENGTHENING, SUPPLING	130
SKIP JUMPING, STANDING TAKE-OFF	130
ARM AND SHOULDER, PIKE	131
TUCK	131
TWIST, BALANCE	132
STRENGTHENING	133
SUPPLING	133
SPRINGBOARD RUN AND HURDLE STEP	133
NECK AND HEAD, ARMS AND SHOULDERS	134
PIKE	134
BACKWARD ROLL TUCK	135
STRENGTHENING	135
SUPPLING, DEPLETIVE	136
EXERCISE FOR A FLYING FORWARD SOMERSAULT	138

ACKNOWLEDGEMENTS

In presenting this 1966 edition of '*Diving Instruction*' I should like to thank all those who have assisted. I appreciate the help and constructive criticism of my colleagues on the A.S.A. Diving Committee, in particular its former Honorary Secretary, Mr. C. J. Scott, to whom I am also grateful for the Foreword, and to Dr. H. Noel Bleasdale, M.B., Ch.B., who has so ably contributed 'The Medical Aspect of Diving'. I am grateful to John Candler, who was the subject for most of the photographic illustrations, and to Mr. W. Orner for his assistance with these, using a Polaroid Land Camera, and also to Mr. Derek Witty who used a Leningrad 35 m.m. camera. The line drawings have been prepared by Mr. H. A. Graham and Mr. J. Wright. Mr. N. A. Brampton and his colleagues of Educational Productions Ltd., have been a great help to me.

This 1966 edition is virtually a completely new book but I am still indebted to all those who helped with the three previous editions.

Lastly, my thanks to my wife whose patience has made this book possible.

CHAPTER I

TEACHING, COACHING AND CLASS MANAGEMENT

THIS CHAPTER is concerned with the principles of teaching and class management as they apply to diving. The teaching of diving is not regularly attempted in schools and other educational establishments. Indeed, even in most swimming clubs the coaching of diving is restricted, at the present time, to a small number of devoted individuals. It is recognised that to attain full competence in diving, individual coaching is ultimately required, but a great deal may be done in schools and other places to encourage the art and to establish the basic movements. There must be many hundreds of young people in this country who possess the ability to rise to the highest levels of diving and who yet have had no opportunity to practise the art or to receive even the most basic instruction in it.

The comments in this chapter, whilst they are concerned essentially with teaching, can be applied equally to coaching. The broad principles are much the same; it is only in application and opportunity that they differ.

SKILL ACQUISITION

Regard must be paid to the principles of skill acquisition. Diving is undoubtedly a complicated skill and from the very beginning the principles which govern the learning of this skill should be clearly before teacher and coach. It should be remembered that the whole personality of the individual is involved in acquiring the skill and that each person is unique. Each member of a class differs from the others in many ways: physically, intellectually and emotionally, and problems arising from these differences should be recognised. Furthermore, there is no best method of teaching a skill and no single way is right all the time; methods must be varied to suit the objective, the environment and the personalities of pupils and teacher.

Visual Aids are extremely important. Demonstration, pictorial illustrations, film loops are all required in the process of learning, but they must be accompanied by verbal comment and explanation to have the full effect. Within the bounds of safety it is helpful to provide opportunities for pupils to discover and explore their own natural abilities. In doing so they will gain in confidence and the teacher is provided with an opportunity of assessing their performance. When possible, it is preferable for the pupil to try the full skill first rather than the part practice. In diving this must be tempered by the fact that in progressing the fundamental movements must be first learnt. It would be impossible to attempt a $2\frac{1}{2}$ forward somersault if a $1\frac{1}{2}$ had not been properly learnt.

Once the whole skill has been attempted further practice of the parts can then be appreciated in relation to their effects on the whole movement, and the purpose of these practices properly realised. Repetitive practices provide opportunities of improving skill and they are effective only if they are carefully guided and their purpose understood. It is useless to go on repeating the practice of a dive or a movement unless the pupil realises what he is doing. Throughout the teaching of diving, interest should be maintained and this is particularly so with young children and beginners. Excessive stress on technique, form and scientific background is not required at this stage. Let them by all means think about the movements, but do not bewilder them with masses of theoretical knowledge.

It is essential that the pupil should want to learn and that he can supply a unifying drive through his own interests, motivation or emotional attitudes. By supplying this drive the acquisition of skill will be greatly enhanced.

PLACE OF DIVING IN NORMAL CLASS TEACHING

For most schoolchildren diving can only be a part of a swimming lesson — at the best 10 minutes in a 30 minutes period. Nevertheless, its place in every swimming lesson must be assured because:

1. Children are interested in diving, chiefly because it is individualistic and they like to shine as individuals, but also because it appeals to their sense of daring and achievement.

2. Ability to dive and/or jump from heights is essential to life-saving and diving is, therefore, a necessary part of many Life Saving and Survival Awards.

3. Diving provides a physical exercise of the highest quality calling for strength, suppleness, co-ordination of movement, and courage. Diving can be continued by most children after they leave school, and moreover it is done in hygienic conditions.

In most cases, practice of diving will not advance beyond a plain header from the top board either because of lack of diving facilities or lack of time.

At first, learning to dive goes hand in hand with learning to swim, as outlined in Chapter II. But once the child can dive from the side of the bath it should become a specialised activity, the direct aim of which is not usually connected with the aim of the swimming lesson in particular but only with the general aim of swimming teaching. The vast majority of people associate diving with what is technically a plunge, which is the method of entering the water in reasonable comfort and without obtaining height, from the side of the bath. This is quite different from diving proper which requires that height be gained in take-off and that a vertical entry, or nearly so, should be achieved. It is therefore very necessary at this stage to make it clear to both teachers and pupils that whilst the plunge dive is to be encouraged for recreational and competitive swimming, survival, and indeed life saving purposes, this is not diving proper and as soon as possible they should commence the activities outlined later, which will encourage them to get up into the air from the side of the bath or diving board.

LAND DRILLS

It has been scientifically proved that there is very little transfer of skill from one situation to another. Certainly it would be extremely difficult to simulate on land the movements made during free fall in the air. The muscular actions themselves are entirely different and on many occasions opposite. However, land drills do have a place in diving teaching. The movements required for take-off can be accurately practised on land and a springboard or diving platform is not required for this. But for the dive proper, land drills can only indicate to the diver the sequence of the movements he will ultimately perform in the air. He can analyse these movements mentally but the muscular action in doing them on land bears no relationship to the action produced whilst in the air.

Land drills can play a valuable part in physical education lessons in the gymnasium. The standing take-offs can all be taught from a box or vaulting horse on to mats and the springboard run-up and hurdle step is a good co-ordinating exercise for inclusion in a physical education lesson.

PHASES OF DIVING TEACHING

Schemes of work for diving teaching can only be formulated in accordance with local conditions, such as available facilities, time allocation, the needs of the pupils and staffing; but they should follow (in general) the outline set out here. The first guiding principle is that the teacher must not let his pupils attempt too much in any one lesson nor must he expect perfection at the first few attempts. Furthermore he may find that some pupils improve much more rapidly than others. Work should always be from the known to the unknown, but the good teacher should keep returning to the known to revise and polish. The phases given here assume the existence of normal facilities, e.g. a firm board up to 10 feet and a 1 metre springboard.

PHASES

1. Confidence exercises in the water.
2. Exercises and elementary movements from the bath side.
3. The plain header from the bath side.
4. Jumps and the plain header from the topboard (a max. of 10 feet).

5. The standing springboard take-off.
6. Plain header from the springboard.
7. Tuck dive standing from the springboard.
8. The springboard running take-off.
9. Tuck dive running from the springboard.
10. Back dive from the side of the bath.
11. Back dive from the springboard.

This is normally the limit of activities within normal class tuition. Beyond this stage individual coaching and correction are increasingly necessary because of the variation in pupils' abilities. However, some introduction to more advanced diving may still be given in class tuition. Somersaults can be attempted — both forward and backward — from the side of the bath. Armstands straight can be done from the bath side and also a variety of movements which are described later under the leading up practices for the key dives.

GROUP WORK

The usual number for a swimming class is 30. If diving instruction has to be given with such a class, group work is essential to make the best of the facilities available, and to cater for the varying standards of the pupils.

Once the beginner phase has been passed, the varying abilities of the pupils will be more apparent at every session. The class must, therefore, be grouped according to ability. One word of warning though — the most promising diver must not be taken to the deep end until a swim of at least one length has been completed. To complicate matters, diving ability does not go hand in hand with swimming ability. A class grouped for swimming may have to be re-grouped for diving activities. Only a good knowledge of the class, a clear vision of the various stages of diving, and a realisation of the facilities available, will enable a teacher to group his class successfully.

The teacher must arrange the work to be done in each lesson so that he can teach what is new to one group while the other groups are practising known activities. At the same time, a watchful eye must be kept on these groups and the teacher should personally see every pupil perform some dive in the lesson and comment on it to the pupil, in order to maintain interest and enthusiasm.

Groups should be kept as small as possible, particularly where diving boards are being used. Eight is usually the maximum number of people who can use a 1 metre springboard in succession.

THE TEACHER

Of all teaching, that of diving, particularly of advanced diving, is perhaps the most exacting. The teacher must inspire confidence in his pupils. He has to feel and remove their fears, and confidently urge them on to the next step. It is a strain and a continual giving of emotional activity on the part of the teacher, but it must be done. He must cajole, bully, bribe, sympathise, walk away in apparent disgust, flatter, command, plead and he must never, never give up! The class must feel the teacher is master of every situation and that he knows his subject. The teacher, too, must help his pupils obtain a clear mental picture of what they are about to attempt. Without this picture, the co-ordination and timing of dives are bound to fail. The teacher should especially note the following points:

1. Commands should be concise and clear.
2. A reserve of voice power must be kept for when occasion demands.
3. Pitch and rhythm of voice should indicate the type of work to be done.
4. Work to be done should be carefully prepared.
5. The teacher's place is on the bath side. Adequate control cannot be exercised from anywhere else!

A teacher should try to introduce something new in each session. He must see that all his pupils do eventually use all the facilities available, e.g., that everyone does dive from the top board and the springboard. It is tempting and satisfying to spend too much time with the more advanced pupils, but it usually means the remainder stand around and shiver.

Enthusiasm, confidence and understanding are the essentials of the successful diving teacher.

SIGNALS

The acoustic properties of most baths are poor and with other activities going on there is always a background of noise. A code of signals understood by the class will save the voice and will often prevent the misunderstanding of a half-heard verbal command.

Whistle signals should be used only when necessary. The baths staff dislike a continual serenade on a whistle and with children familiarity breeds contempt! Some usual signals are:

> *One long blast* — stand still wherever you are, or if in deep water go to the side and be quiet.
>
> *Two long blasts* — leave the water.
>
> *A series of short blasts* — get away from the diving boards. Divers remain still.
>
> Hand signals are useful to divers actually on the diving boards.
>
> *Stop sign* — stay where you are.
>
> *Wave on* — do your dive.
>
> *Clenched fist* — with tuck.
>
> *Forefinger and thumb together* — with pike.

DISCIPLINE

Diving discipline should always be firmer than that for swimming. There is a greater need for care and control with diving and discipline must see this is assured. The best

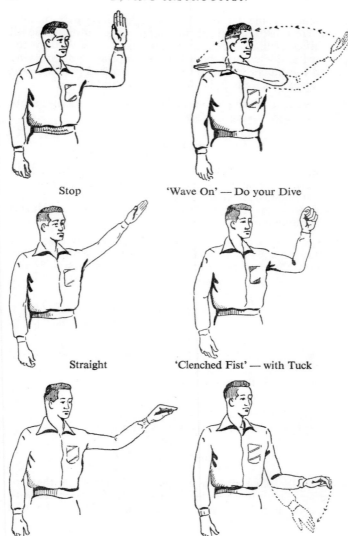

Stop

'Wave On' — Do your Dive

Straight

'Clenched Fist' — with Tuck

'Forefinger and Thumb together' — with Pike   Wait

FIG. 1 — HAND SIGNALS

discipline is a quiet firmness which is felt rather than heard. This firmness must not only be a general atmosphere, it must be carried into the work the class does. When a teacher sets out to teach a particular activity, all the group must attempt it. To allow shirking means a loss in prestige on the part of the teacher and a weakening in the confidence of the pupil.

On the other hand a proper respect for all diving activities must be instilled; a casual approach to them may well lead to accidents.

Some points essential to discipline are listed below:

1. Rigorously prevent 'cross swimming' under the diving board.
2. When a diver is doing movements with a backward take-off, see no one moves across his line of vision.
3. Never allow horse-play or fooling on the diving boards.
4. Never allow pushing-in.
5. See that all signals are implicitly obeyed.
6. Never allow two people on the springboard at the same time. It spoils the recoil and eventually ruins the board.
7. When advanced dives are being done see that there is no unnecessary noise in the bath which will distract the diver.

The divers must be confident in the signals and control of the teacher when diving from the boards. If the diver is at all worried as to the movements of others he cannot dive correctly.

Under the all-seeing eye of the teacher, opportunity for free diving should be given in each lesson. Pupils should be able to play and express themselves, experiment if they wish. The teacher will learn much by watching!

In many baths there is a physical separation between the diving pit and the remainder of the swimming pool. This may vary from a simple rope or a line of floats stretched across the bath, to a movable boom, or, in the most refined stage, to a separate diving pit. Some means of separation will certainly ease the problem of the teacher in controlling a mixed class of swimmers and divers or where he has also to accommodate members of the general public. Unquestionably all baths in the future will have some form of separation.

HYGIENE

This aspect must never be neglected by bath users! The use of lavatories, showers and foot-baths is absolutely necessary. There are other factors too which are most important to a diver.

Bathing costumes

These should be clean and well fitting. They are very important to the general impression a diver gives in a competition. Men's trunks should be snugly fitting and a jock-strap worn by male divers doing advanced dives. Ladies' costumes are best made of Lastex or some similar stretching material. Above all see that costumes or trunks are comfortable.

Hair

This should be cut short or a bathing hat worn. Hair falling over the eyes and obscuring the vision is very dangerous.

Toe Nails

These should be cut short and square. A long nail is softened by water and easily broken or torn during diving.

Feet

They are best kept hard after water work by rubbing with methylated spirit. Diving with tender feet can be a torture!

Ear plugs

These are often needed by advanced divers working above 1 metre. Any undue discomfort caused by water rushing up the nose in feet-first entries can be counteracted by nose-clips. On no account should nose or ears be stuffed with cotton wool and medical advice should be obtained before using ear plugs and nose clips.

First Aid

See that the baths have a complete outfit. The teacher, too, ought to have a knowledge of the fundamentals of First Aid.

Soreness

A little olive oil or vaseline rubbed into the skin will prevent soreness often caused by waiting wet on a board in a wind when open-air diving. Care, too, should be taken to avoid sunburn. Take open-air diving in small measures at first.

AIDS TO TEACHING

The good teacher will leave no avenue unexplored to further the aims of his teaching. There are many aids to the teaching of diving which not only stimulate the interest of the pupils but also provide further knowledge of the subject and in some cases practice of movements done whilst diving.

The film loop

A most useful aid to diving is the film loop. By this means the world's greatest divers and the most complicated dives can be brought immediately to the pupil and where it is possible to have a film projector set up on or near the bath surround, the pupil can absorb between dives the movement he is about to attempt. This aid requires a good deal of development as yet but it is a medium which every teacher must explore and use. Film loops are cheap and easily made and projectors not too expensive. The latest type of projector (800E, made by Technicolor) has a daylight screen and can be used on the bath surround with ease. The pupils can see the dive split into its component parts, see the sequence of movements and absorb them into the mind immediately before going on the board to attempt that dive. This mental preparation for a dive is the most important factor in learning any new dive or movement. It saves a great deal of talk and leaves the pupils in no doubt as to what is expected of them.

Video-tape recorder

This is an expensive but tremendously useful aid. Using what looks like a small cine-camera the coach can take a video-recording of a diver in action. This can be played back immediately and shown on a small television screen. The diver and his coach can see exactly what has been done. The recording can be slowed down and a stopped action picture presented if required. Provided that normal electrical safeguards regarding earthing, etc., are carried out, the apparatus can be safely used on the bath side.

Diving photographs and wallcharts

These are a similar help but the progression of movement is not the same as with a film loop. Pupils, however, should be encouraged to make collections of diving photographs to stimulate interest. An expensive but most useful aid is a Polaroid Camera whereby a photograph can be taken of a dive and produced in a few moments on the bath side.

There are now a number of wallcharts available which illustrate many of the basic movements in diving.

Exhibitions of diving

These are excellent in encouraging would-be divers and provide a standard at which to aim, but it is doubtful whether youngsters learn anything of the movements involved. It takes a trained observer to note even the essentials of the many things a diver does during an advanced dive.

The sandpit

This usually consists of a 1 metre springboard projecting over a pit approximately 2 feet deep, 5 feet wide and 10 feet long filled with dry sand. The springboard may be 1 metre or slightly more above the level of the sand, which enables physical support to be given by standers-by when, for example, a reversed somersault is attempted for the first time. On the other hand it may be a mere foot above the level of the sand, which makes the diver attempt all his movements in the air above the board. From the springboard, movements with feet-first entries can be practised in safety. The chief benefit is that there is no contact with cold and chilling water and hence practice in track suit or sweater can go on for much longer than with water work. Moreover, all the movements, except those of entry, are identical with those performed from the actual diving board. With the 'entry' or landing, the diver must bend forward at the knees and hips at the moment of landing and place the arms out sideways in case of slipping to one side.

Preliminary practice in forward rolls and shoulder rolls should be given before commencing sandpit work so that should the diver go over in his feet first landing he may roll forward on to the sand. Should the diver feel he is falling backwards on landing, the easiest and safest thing is for him to sit down on the sand with the arms out sideways.

Undoubtedly the sandpit's greatest use is in the practice of take-offs. Work done on the sandpit need not necessarily be repeated immediately from the diving board but the teacher must remember that all work learnt on the sandpit must be applied in actual diving and that sandpit work is only an aid to the teaching of diving.

The trampoline

This consists of a rectangular metal frame with canvas stretched on to it by means of elastic rope or steel springs. The energy used by the performer in depressing the 'bed' is returned during its recoil. This bed gives considerable spring and by bouncing on it, good height may be obtained in the air and diving movements attempted during this 'flight'. Where there is at least 12 feet headroom, the trampoline can be used indoors and thus provide divers with training opportunities when baths are not available. As with the sandpit, practice can go on much longer than with actual diving.

In using a trampoline it is essential that the performer first learns all the various methods of take-off and landing on the trampoline. The performer may then go on to practise all dives with feet first entries, and even those with head first entries, provided that in doing so he has perfected a landing which allows him to fall face downwards on to the canvas, where, with arms bent, palms downwards, he can absorb the recoil.

Somersaulting and twisting belts suspended from pulleys over the trampoline may allow the learner to appreciate the feel of an entire movement in absolute safety, and a stander-by, controlling the ropes of this apparatus, can arrest the performer's descent on to the 'bed'.

A running springboard take-off can be simulated by placing a firm approach board up to the edge of the trampoline supported at the other end by, for example, a gymnasium wall bar, so that the board lies horizontal. The approach is made along the board and the hurdle step is taken at the end of the board supported by the trampoline frame, the diver alighting on to the bed which operates as the end of a springboard. The diver will thus be able to practise the complete take-off. It is essential that his landing occurs in the middle of the bed to give an adequate safety margin in all directions.

Another way to simulate the springboard approach is to start with one foot on the frame and the other foot on the edge of the bed, take one step forward and jump into a hurdle, taking off from the bed to land as near the centre of the trampoline as possible. Throughout all trampoline work it must be stressed that standers-by are imperative; there ought to be one pupil standing by at each side of the frame and should the performer slip, or lose his direction, the stander-by can firmly push him back on to the bed.

Care should be taken when dismounting from the trampoline. Do not jump straight on to the floor, it will feel strangely hard after the trampoline bed! Instead, grasp the frame at one corner and after placing one foot on it, neatly step off to land on both feet alongside the frame, maintaining your grasp, until balance has been achieved.

A disadvantage is that trampoline work can develop into a form of acrobatics removed from diving. Also, after trampoline work, a springboard feels dead and lifeless. The best way to use the trampoline is to alternate between this and actual springboard diving in the pool. This practice must not, however, be in the same session but divided into trampolining one evening and diving the following.

The trampette

The trampette is a smaller edition of the trampoline and can be most useful to a diver. The metal frame is sloping and about four feet square. It can be used in a gymnasium where mats are available for landing on, outside with a sandpit, or on the bath side with entries into the water.

Unlike the trampoline the run-up and hurdle step can be easily practised along a marked out bench or form leading up to the trampette's lower edge. It is extremely easy to teach a somersault — either forward or backward — with this apparatus and a stander-by can be placed near enough to the performer to assist if required. It is light and easily portable.

Bath side run up

A useful aid for practising firmboard take-offs is a 'run-up', laid on the side of the bath. This should take the form of a strip of non-slip material, similar in size and material to that which is used on the firmboard. A diver can then practise a great number of take-offs in a very short time indeed and save himself the trouble of climbing up to the firmboard.

Underwater windows

These are becoming increasingly common in new bath construction and if placed opposite the points of entry from diving boards, allow the coach to study entry techniques.

DEPTHS OF WATER

Few teachers will have the use of really adequate diving facilities, but rarely are facilities at hand so poor that some diving instruction cannot be given. The good teacher must therefore have a knowledge of the depths and areas of water and height of boards necessary for safe diving.

If proper teaching in diving is to be given it must be remembered that vertical entries are essential, therefore an adequate depth of water must always be present to obtain a true vertical entry. The depths of water required for championships are set out in the 'Manual on Diving' but it may well be that a little less can be accepted by the teacher or the coach, having regard to the physical characteristics of his pupils; for example, a plain header from the side of the bath requires at least 8 feet of water for a normal man who, with arms outstretched above his head, will just be touching the bottom of the bath as his feet disappear under the surface. As he dives from higher up he will hit the water with much greater momentum and therefore he requires either a shallower entry or more water in which to absorb the momentum of his movement. Broadly speaking, it would appear that children up to junior school age can perform the plain header from the bath side quite safely into 5 feet of water. Up to fourteen years of age they certainly require a minimum of 6 feet, and for heights above the bath side, including the 1 metre springboard, a minimum of 8 feet 6 inches is absolutely essential. Adults require 9 feet 10 inches in depth of water for 1 metre springboard diving.

Where running dives are to be performed from firmboards the teacher should ensure that the boards permit four running paces and that the ends are free from all rails and projections. All firmboards should project at least 3 feet over the water up to 5 metres high and 6 feet after that.

In open-air pools the diver ought not to perform with the sun shining directly into his eyes. In indoor baths all artificial lighting should be above the diver. Under-water illumination is bad for diving and the water surface should never be absolutely still and smooth. The water surface under a diving board should be agitated by spraying water on to it or by forcing air through it. This requirement is now an essential fitting in all modern baths.

THE COACH

Advanced diving teaching can only be given in the form of coaching, preferably one coach with one diver at a time. Once pupils begin work on the springboard they progress at vastly different rates and along different lines. Coaching is the only way to give adequate teaching. Where correction has to be given to an advanced diver it cannot be readily applied if the pupil has to queue for his turn on the diving board. The coach dealing with one or two pupils can avoid this. As dives become more difficult, more time must be spent on each one and the coach must enter more into the personality of the diver.

Necessary as coaching is — here are some words of warning.

First, youth today is becoming 'coach conscious'. Young people will not, and apparently cannot, work without the presence and stimulation of a coach. Perhaps coaches are over-enthusiastic and are in some measure responsible for this condition. However, a coach must induce into his pupils a capacity for work with or without his presence and point out very forcibly that it is the diver, *not* the coach, who is training. Whilst no diver can aspire to great heights without a coach, divers must spend as much time in practice on their own as with their coach.

Coaches must remember too that they are not mere 'fault observers' and 'correctors'. They must find out what is most suitable for their pupils and lead them along the chosen paths. Rigid regimentation is not required and the wise coach should allow his pupils to experiment and suggest for themselves.

A weakening in respect and discipline often occurs between coach and pupil. Although the familiarity of their association is much closer than with a teacher and his class, the coach must still retain the power of command and control. At the final issue his word must be law. Too many coaches eventually degenerate into personal attendants carrying a large supply of towels.

Coaching is in many respects more difficult than class teaching. The stimuli of class work, discipline and enthusiasm are gone. On the other hand the coach should know his pupils 'inside-out', and be able to vary his teaching with the mood of the pupils.

Coaching is often an exasperating and disappointing task, but remember, it takes two to make a bargain — the fault may not always lie with the ineptitude of the pupil. A coach must develop the ability of self analysis and criticism.

Despite the pitfalls in coaching, it can be, and often is, a satisfying and invigorating form of teaching. Results are often quickly obtained and cause and effect are easily related.

Coaching procedure

Each coach will naturally have his own methods of approach and teaching and these will no doubt vary from pupil to pupil and occasion to occasion. Some outlines are given here of suggested coaching procedure, but there can be no hard and fast rules.

Amount of work

Diving practice should take place as often as possible, providing the pupil does not become bored and stale and that he receives adequate rest and change of activities. A diver in training should train 5 or 6 days a week, and 2 or 3 days a week during the off-season.

Duration of workouts

Much will depend on the facilities, the weather conditions and the opportunities and physique of the diver, but the ideal of 2 one-hourly periods of training a day should be aimed at.

The general outline of a workout should be as follows:

1. Warming up on land.
2. Take-off practice on land.
3. Take-off practice on board.
4. Practice of simple dives.
5. Practice of simpler dives leading up to new dive about to be learnt (e.g., for flying forward somersault C (with tuck) practise forward dive straight and forward somersault C).
6. The new dive.
7. Free practice of known dives.

With new dives, pre-diving exercises should be done as set out in 'Exercises for Divers', Chapter IX, page 127.

'Advanced Coaching'

When a diver is approaching the standard of National competition, more specialised coaching is required, and the emphasis moves from learning new dives to acquiring polish to those already known. New dives should be learnt outside the competitive period and the coach plans his work accordingly. He should have a scheme which over a period of years brings his diver to those dives with the maximum tariff value compatible with the diver's physical and mental capabilities. New dives done in competition this year should be the basis of more advanced ones next, e.g., a reverse dive half twist should become a reverse dive half twist one-and-a-half somersaults. Dives with no real development, such as the one twist backward, should not be used, when training with even a slightly lower tariff dive will prepare the technique for more advanced dives. Similarly, it is a waste of time to bring numerous dives up to competitive standard. Make a programme and stick to it.

When a competition is approaching, the diver should practise his dives at first in group order, i.e., the dives from the forward group then those from the reverse group and so on, doing all the running movements before the standing ones. Later, in at least the last fortnight, dives should be done in competition order. In this period only movements executed very badly should be repeated before going on to the next dive, the training should be 'geared' to repeating the sequence. Any really weak dives should receive separate treatment at the end of the sequence training, but do not overdo it — all such training ought to end on a high note with a better dive. Knowing when to stop is the coach's greatest attribute.

Where a diver is doing both springboard and firmboard, do the springboard training first in any session, but best of all separate the work into two sessions if possible.

The results of competitions should be very carefully analysed by both coach and diver. The record of marks scored should always be obtained from the official recorder, or if these are not made available then the coach must keep his own. It is only from a strict analysis of the results of several competitions that a coach may truly evaluate the dives his pupil is using in competitions. The choice so far has been at the discretion of the coach and diver, but on entering competitions such analysis may provide another yardstick and the judges' views may well influence the diver in his future programme and choice of dives.

Remember that diving is more mental than physical work. Observations at the A.S.A. Diving School show that four to four and a half hours actual diving a day, no matter how well interspaced, is the limit for any diver, with even less if all from 10 metres.

Fault correction

Fault finding and correction is perhaps 50 per cent. of a coach's work. The chief difficulty is to keep it creative. It is all too easy to criticise without really helping the pupils. It is useless to find fault if methods of correction are not suggested. The coach must also possess a knowledge of the basic mechanics of diving. He must know where the dive went wrong and why, if he is to give a lasting correction.

The coach must always have a clear picture in his mind of his idea of the perfect dive, jump or movement and he must try to transfer it to the minds of the pupils.

The coach must never pick faults for talking's sake. It is not necessary to find fault with every dive. Indeed, although a dive may not be perfect insomuch as more polish, control and finish are required, the dive may be fundamentally correct and require no correction of any point but only continued practice.

Perfection is not quickly attained and the coach should not be too hard with his pupils. All faults cannot be corrected at once and a dismal recitation of every fault a diver has committed in a dive is not encouraging. It is preferable to deal with one fault at a time.

It is not good coaching to persevere too long to correct a fault or poor dive. Pupils often lose confidence in themselves. If the fault or dive does not seem to come right, leave it until the pupil has gone back to better-known fundamental movements and restored his confidence. The fault may even be left to a later lesson provided it is eventually mastered and not hedged time and time again.

Fault correction is mostly done by explaining how the fault can be avoided, e.g., if the head in a dive is too far forward, move it back to its proper position. Other errors may be due to faulty fundamental positions and the best of divers needs constant practice of all the various stages of diving technique. A good physical condition will do much to help. Toes not pointed in a dive usually indicates poor ankle mobility. Knees bent in a pike position may mean short ham-string muscles.

A coach should endeavour to see every dive as a whole and

not just isolated movements. When in doubt always go back to the take-off from whence most faults originate.

The most common faults are dealt with in the appropriate chapters of this book.

'Knocks'

The teacher or coach must appreciate that, even with the best-ordered teaching, accidents do occur. It is the prime responsibility of the teacher to reduce the risk of accident to a minimum, but, nevertheless, he must be prepared to accept some as inevitable, particularly when teaching new dives.

The commonest 'knock' is for the diver to hit the water when not in an entry position, e.g. whilst still balled up when doing somersaults or flat on the back when not getting the height necessary to attain the correct entry position from a back movement. Water is hard! It stings, shocks and often stuns. After such a knock the diver should be encouraged to go back and attempt the dive again, after receiving the necessary verbal corrections. To delay or put off may mean a loss of confidence on the part of the pupil and coach.

The coach has to be hard-hearted to achieve his goal. Sympathy can be very much misplaced. Praise after the dive has been successfully attempted is more important than ministrations over a faulty movement.

By far the worst 'knock' is to hit the board during a dive. Where the knock is only slight and the diver can continue, the coach should be very searching in his enquiry into why the accident occurred. Should he have any doubt as to the ability or technique of the diver he must not repeat the dive until he has thoroughly gone through all the building up stages again.

The teacher is responsible for the safety of his pupils but he must not be soft and over-anxious. A firm confident outlook by the coach will do much to stimulate the diver. If the coach wavers or shows fear, it will be repeated manifold by the diver. The coach has often to appear cruel to be kind.

Competitions

The teacher may find it difficult due to the facilities at hand, to stimulate interest by means of competition. Where a one metre springboard is available most children before the end of their normal school career should be able to perform at least three movements — whether jumps or dives — from it. This provides the basis for a school or junior club competition. Allow the contestants a free choice and do not, as in competitive diving proper, count dives of the same number in the International Tariff, as the same dive; e.g., a competitor could do a Forward Dive in Tuck, in Pike and Straight, as his three dives.

Where only firmboards exist do not restrict the competition to Plain headers, allow the contestants a choice of both movements and heights from which to perform them, consistent with safe depths of water. Where only the bath side can be used the same freedom should follow. A competitor might well perform, a Forward Dive with Tuck, a Handstand Straight and a Back Dive Straight. Encourage the pupils to have a real attempt at diving, allow them to experiment. If need arises the teacher should draw up his own tariff starting with the Plain header from the bath side ranking as 1.0.

Such competitions as these will not only stimulate the interest of the pupils in diving but awaken that of their audience too!

CHAPTER 11

STARTING TO DIVE

FOR THE BEGINNER learning to dive should be an accompaniment to learning to swim. The preliminary practices for both activities give the pupil confidence in the water, the new element to be experienced. In the early stages, children seem to regard diving just as a means of getting into the water and surfacing as quickly as possible in order to swim. They enter the water usually with a flat plunge dive which, later on, serves as the foundation for a good racing dive. However, in order to encourage children in diving as an art, the teacher should develop this tendency to gain a quick head-first entry by encouraging the pupils to gain more height from the starting position in an effort to produce a more nearly vertical entry. These are essential requirements in competitive diving.

As soon as the beginner can enter the water head first, with confidence, he will soon learn to differentiate between the two types of dives which can be developed together.

Having practised the early confidence exercises for swimming, fear of water should have been removed and the earliest diving practices should be found easy to perform. However, for easy reference and to stress their importance early exercises relating to diving are presented here.

It must not be assumed that a child who cannot dive must be taken through the full range of these practices or follow the same sequence. The more adventurous and able child may dive immediately with no formal teaching. The practices given are in a progressive sequence for ease of understanding but the teacher should choose only those necessary to help the individual child.

Earliest Stages—Shallow End

1. Head bobbing under water. Pupils hold the rail, keeping eyes open and blowing out bubbles. Do not allow pupils to hold noses or on resurfacing to wipe eyes and faces. With the children in pairs they can take it in turn to bob under the water to see how many fingers their partners are showing.

FIG. 2—PUSH AND GLIDE (SEE PARAGRAPH 5 BELOW)

2. Picking up objects from the floor of the bath. Again pupils are becoming used to submersion and to opening eyes under water, essential in diving.

3. Jumping in with and without support. This can be done in the very first lesson. Pupils should be in pairs, one supporting or catching the other. Style in the jump is not important; it is essentially a confidence exercise.

4. Push and glide. This should be carried out by first pushing to the bath side and then away from the side to a partner. Emphasis must be on keeping the face in the water with the head pressed between the arms during the glide.

5. Push and glide to the bottom of the bath. Teach return to the surface by bending the hands so that fingers point upwards and by raising the head. Palms of the hands must face downwards in all gliding practices. Never allow palms to be together. This could be a dangerous practice in subsequent diving entries.

6. Push and glide between a partner's legs.

7. Push and glide from the steps in the shallow end. Start from the bottom step and work up until the feet are on or just above water line. The beginner should crouch on the step, toes curled round the edge and with the arms extended beyond the head, upper arms pulled close in to the ears. This can be done with partner support at first, the beginner pushing out to his partner 6 to 10 feet away. Emphasise the 'push' and stimulate this by competition for distance.

Practices from the Bath Side into Shallow Water

From activities in the water, pupils can proceed to practices from the bath side into the water between 3 and 5 feet deep.

FIG. 3 — THE SITTING DIVE

The Sitting Dive

Pupils sit on the edge of the bath as near to the edge as possible. Feet rest on the rail or scum channel, arms are raised in front to almost shoulder height pointing slightly downwards to the water, palms downwards, upper arms pressed close in to the ears; the knees are together, head is dropped forward chin on chest and the chest as near to the knees as is comfortable. Pupils over-balance and push forward and downward into the water. Encourage the pupils to keep their heads down between their arms. The class can work in pairs at first, one supporting the other in the water. Emphasis should be on the distance across the bath achieved by the pupils in the plunge position, face in the water.

The Crouch Dive

This is almost the same as the Sitting Dive but the starting position allows for a more vigorous extension of hips, knees and ankles. Pupils crouch at the bath side, toes gripping the edge, feet and legs together, knees bent, arms beyond head pointing slightly downwards, chin on chest. Pupils should over-balance and push hard from the feet and fall forward into the water. The crouch position should be gradually straightened out in successive practices until the pupils attain the position normally taken in a racing start dive but with arms extended beyond the head and close to the ears.

FIG. 4 — THE CROUCH DIVE

The Lunge Dive

This is not always a necessary dive but it may be useful with pupils who experience difficulty in over-balancing in the final stages of the crouch dive. Pupils stand with one leg behind the other in an informal lunge position. Toes of the forward leg are curled round tha bath edge. This leg is bent at the knee, rear leg is straight. Arms are raised beyond and almost in line with the upper body, chin is on chest. Pupils push from the forward knee and foot and bring their legs together in the air for entry. It should be attempted with alternate legs forward.

The Plunge Dive

Here the pupil takes up the stance as for the final stages of the crouch dive except that the arms hang loosely down from the shoulder. As the body overbalances and begins to fall towards the water, the arms are swung vigorously forward beyond and in line with the body, and the legs push away from the bath side. During flight the body should be as straight and as streamlined

FIG. 5 — THE LUNGE DIVE

as possible and the entry should be made at an angle of between 14 and 20 degrees to the water. The streamlined stretched position of flight is continued under the water and by raising the hands and head slightly the swimmer will return to the surface. The aim must be to get as far as possible without swimming a stroke. Until the swimmer wishes to surface the head must be kept down in to what is in fact, the normal position if the body were standing erect.

This plunge dive can be readily adapted to suit the racing start dive for any prone stroke.

Common Faults and their Correction
1. An unbalanced starting position such as standing precariously on the toes. Emphasise a sound stance, feet flat, toes over the edge.
2. The beginner lacking in confidence may fall into the water with no thrust. Restore confidence by returning to earlier practices.
3. Hands apart on entry. Emphasise hands touching palms facing downwards.
4. Head raised causing a flat entry; usually due to lack of confidence. Return to earlier confidence practices.
5. Pulling the hands to the sides as soon as the body enters the water. This may be dangerous as the hands can no longer protect the head. Emphasise holding the glide position.

Free Jumps

The practice of informal standing jumps should be continued mainly as confidence exercises. On no account must there be any attempt to teach form in take-off. Pupils may try 'who can jump farthest from the bath side?' or 'who can jump the highest?'.

THE PLAIN HEADER

The pupils are now entering the water head first with confidence; in other words, they can dive to swim. Instruction should now be given for diving in the aesthetic sense. The easiest and most useful preliminary dive for this is the plain header.

For years, we have used the English header in this country as our basic dive, but it has in fact been proved a most difficult dive to perform as laid down and moreover it has been performed largely by various unorthodox methods, e.g., by piking (bending at the hips during flight) and by bending the arms up in front of the body in the take-off swing. Furthermore the English header does not assist more advanced diving as it encourages 'topple' rather than a push up through the hips, thereby encouraging beginners in a fault very difficult to overcome.

The plain header is easy to learn, it embodies the correct elements of diving progression, and it can be performed from the bath side, even by adults, into only eight feet of water. Provided that the water depth is satisfactory it can be performed up to and including a 10 feet high firmboard.

Stages of Teaching

1. In the water at the shallow end.
   - (a) Stand and stretch the arms up in line with the body. Bend the knees, drop the head forward and spring up from the floor of the bath and attempt to dive into the water. Bending at the hips will assist in gaining a head first entry.

FIG. 6 — THE PLAIN HEADER

B*

(*b*) To encourage spring and upward thrust the above exercise can be done by diving over a partner's back, or over a partner's outstretched arms held at water level.

2. From the bath side into 5 feet of water at least.

Stand on the side, toes curled round the edge with feet together. The arms should be extended beyond the head in line with the trunk, and slightly wider than shoulder width apart with palms facing forwards. The body should then be bent forwards at the hips into a slight pike-position. The take-off is made by bending the knees and ankles and then quickly straightening them with a vigorous upward push through the original line of the hips, whilst the upper body is directed downwards and slightly outwards towards the water. This movement is referred to as a pike push.

The point of entry should be noted and in subsequent dives, attempts made to enter nearer and nearer to the bath side. As confidence increases stress must be placed on neatness of execution. Toes must be pointed, legs together and in every dive the entry must be carried to the bottom of the bath. The dive should be done with less and less initial pike until the diver is almost upright in the starting position. The pupils have arrived now at the stage of the plain header.

Ready Position

The diver takes up an erect position on the bath side, toes gripping the edge, heels together. He raises his arms above his head in line with his body and just more than shoulder width apart. Palms are facing forward, thumb and fingers together. The position should be firm and balanced without any suggestion of strain. Eyes should be directed to a point just above head level. In profile, the arms, shoulder and trunk are in the same plane.

Take-off

The knees bend slightly and the shoulders move forward a little, while the weight of the body is moving forward on to the balls of the feet, but the hips must be vertically over the feet. The knees straighten quickly and there is a vigorous extension of the feet. The push must be upwards through the hips. Care should be taken not to allow the arms to move forward and downward out of line with the trunk.

Flight

Apart from a slight bending and then straightening at the hips there should be no movement of body and limbs during flight through the air. The body line should follow the curve of the line of flight, straightening as entry is approached. Arms are kept straight and come together gradually for the entry, at which point the thumbs are touching.

Entry

The desired angle depends on the height of the dive and the angle of take-off. A vertical entry should always be the aim; on no account should the body pass beyond the vertical. A dive less steep than 30 degrees from the vertical must be regarded as unsatisfactory.

The fingers meet the water first, making the initial hole through which the body passes. The top of the head (not the forehead) follows. The body straightens out from its curve as the hands touch the water and stretches hard and firm towards the bottom of the bath. Toes must be pointed. The dive is not complete until the whole of the body has disappeared under the water.

Control

The speed of rotation during the flight may be controlled by moving the arms downward towards the hips (faster) or upwards as for entry (slower), or by increasing or decreasing the bend at the hips. These are, however, corrective movements only and it is frequently found that even with a beginner a faulty take-off will be instinctively corrected by one or other of these movements or a combination of both.

'Judging Notes'

Where the plain header is used in competitions the rules below may be applied. The points should be awarded from 0—10 in increments of $\frac{1}{2}$ points and the dive judged as a whole, not divided into parts for separate marking. The judge should look for the following main features.

1. That reasonable height is obtained in take-off.

2. That a smooth flight is achieved without undulations or excessive bend at the hips.

3. That the entry is near to, but does not exceed, the vertical.

It should be noted that when used in competition, the dive does not vary from the foregoing description. The dive starts when a diver takes up his starting position and is completed when the body is fully submerged. The method of approach to the starting position is at the option of the diver and for judging purposes should be ignored.

Where a diver restarts after commencing his take-off (that is, the arms are returned to the starting position with the body erect), the judges should mark out of 10 and then deduct 2 marks before displaying their award. Failure on a second attempt would count as a failed dive with no points awarded.

When a diver performs or attempts to perform the English header the judge should award points according to the performance seen.

Where the entry is beyond the vertical, points should be deducted by the judges according to their opinion.

If a referee has been appointed for the diving competition, he will make the deduction of 2 points for the restart described above but in many school contests there may not be a referee appointed.

The teacher should give his pupils every encouragement to see more advanced dives and not regard the plain header as the sole dive for school competition. The forward tuck dive can be performed from the bath side and is the next easiest basic diving movement to progress to.

Common Faults and their Corrections

Faults *in the Ready Position*

Bad posture—head bent forward or strained backward; chest or abdomen thrust out; knees bent; feet wide apart; standing with arms out of the body line or too wide apart or too close together; fingers apart.

Corrections

Individuals can correct all these faults in front of a mirror. Standing with the back against a wall helps. Verbal correction by the teacher, together with a good demonstration, should eliminate these faults. The position must be firm and yet without strain.

Faults *in the Take-off*

1. Allowing the arms to come forward out of line with the trunk.
2. Allowing the head to fall forward.
3. Excessive bending of the knees.
4. Poising on the toes.
5. Lack of upward thrust.
6. Not gaining adequate height.
7. Holding the bent knee position before initiating the up-thrust.

Corrections

A good demonstration is invaluable. Emphasize that the eyes should be directed to a distant point, just above eye-level. Stress the quick knee bend and extension and the push UP through the hips. Go back to preliminary practices if the pupil does not push. Springing up practices on land will help to strengthen the muscles used in take-off. Good height must be emphasized.

Faults *in Flight*

1. Hollowing of the back.
2. Lifting the head back.
3. Arms not in line with the body.
4. Opening the legs.
5. Bending the knees.
6. Toes not pointed.
7. Slackness of the body.
8. Twisting of the body.

Corrections

Remember that it is the take-off which is all important. The curve of the line of flight is governed by the angle of take-off and the push imparted. Twisting usually denotes an unequal push from the feet. The position of the limbs, however, is governed by the diver and it is essential that he should present a well defined body curve. Verbal correction and concentration on one point at a time is necessary. Whatever the diver does with his limbs during flight cannot affect his line of flight which is determined at take-off.

Faults *on Entry*

1. Going over.
2. Going in flat.
3. Allowing the body and limbs to crumple as the water is reached.
4. Hollowing the back or turning up the hands under water before the toes are submerged (i.e., attempting to surface too soon).
5. Legs apart.
6. Toes not pointed.
7. Arms, body and legs not in the same straight line.

Corrections

Undue lean in take-off will cause the diver to go over and insufficient rotation imparted to the body at take-off will cause it to go flat. Faults here should be corrected at their source.

The diver must stretch for entry and be encouraged to go to the bottom of the bath. Attempting to surface too soon may result from lack of confidence. Under-water games and swimming will help to cure this.

Verbal corrections should be sufficient to correct faulty limb positions. Emphasize that the eyes should be open.

Free diving

Pupils should be encouraged to dive in as often and as freely as possible now. Where the bath side allows, informal running dives should be permitted, care should be taken, however, to see there is no danger of slipping on the run up. The pupils should now regard diving as the natural means of entry into water, and should enjoy doing it.

Free jumps

Practice of informal jumps should be continued. Pupils may try 'who can jump the farthest from the bath side?' or 'who can jump the highest?' The 'depth charge' is another usual confidence exercise, and is a good preliminary to tuck positions. Pupils jump from the bath side and in mid-air bring the knees up to the chest and grasp them tightly with the arms. This position is held until the entry is completed. The pupils will delight in the amount of splash they can make. The 'depth charge' can be done backwards as well as forwards.

In all these practices the 'follow my leader' method can be used. See, however, that your leaders are good ones! The hesitance of a poor leader is infectious to those who are coming behind.

CHAPTER III

THE SPRINGBOARD

DIVING from a springboard offers the greatest thrills and aesthetic satisfaction of all forms of diving. It brings the art of diving to its most complex and intricate level. With a flexible springboard a diver may cheat the pull of gravity for a little while and perform movements during the upward flight of the body. Indeed, a good springboard diver should have completed most if not all of his dive before he passes the board on his downward way to the water. Springboard diving necessitates control not only of the body and limbs but also of the very instrument used to obtain height — the springboard itself!

As soon as pupils have mastered the plain header from the side, it has been the custom in this country to continue with the plain diving from heights before commencing springboard work. This has been due in part to the lack of springboard facilities but nothing is more certain than that if good springboard diving is to be really mastered, it must begin as early as possible — certainly before the diver becomes too accustomed to diving from firm boards. The plain header should have given the pupil the elements of flight control and entry; he must now master the springboard and know clearly why he is using it. It will provide him with the key which opens the doors to all diving.

Before starting springboard work, pupils should be given a clear picture of why it is used — *to obtain height from the board*! It is not to run off — it is to jump from! Older pupils will soon realise, too, that in obtaining height the body is longer in the air — giving more time to perform movements.

Throughout his career the diver must keep in mind this idea of *height*. It is the chief essential of springboard diving. Other essentials in the use of a springboard are:

1. The diver must go with the board and not against it. As the board goes down or up the diver must adjust his movements to go with it.

2. The take-off must be as near the end of the board as possible in order to obtain the maximum leverage. This can easily be demonstrated with a ruler as the springboard, a pencil as the fulcrum, one hand as the pivot and a small ball of paper as the diver.

3. There must be as little movement forward from the board as possible — up! UP! UP! The further the diver goes forward the less height he obtains.

THE STANDING TAKE-OFF

Springboard diving should begin with the forward standing take-off from a 1-metre board. Pupils are anxious to try springboard diving and long explanations on land are wasted on youngsters straining to try their prowess on a new medium.

Land drill practice of the take-off is an essential preliminary but it should be brief, and followed immediately by practice on the board. At first, entry into the water should be feet-first as in a plain jump, and later head-first by doing a plain header. But the emphasis must be on the take-off and the securing of height. No definite effort should be made at the beginning to teach either a plain jump or a plain header from the springboard. At this stage it is not necessary to correct other faults providing the entry is satisfactory.

The stance

The body should be erect with arms straight and close to the sides. The heels should be touching but the feet may be slightly apart with the toes gripping the edge of the board. Once this position has been comfortably attained the arms may be raised forward and upward to the level of the shoulders, approximately shoulder width apart with palms facing downward. This is a purely optional position but it may assist the diver to obtain balance on the board. Each arm should be in a straight line from the shoulder to the tips of the fingers without being strained and if this position is not comfortable the arms can be opened a little wider. From this balanced position the arms are lowered to the sides. It is when the arms move from here that the dive is judged to have commenced. The movement from the initial stance, if adopted, is not judged.

The take-off

1. *The Preparatory Arm Swing*

From the starting position, with the arms at the sides, the board is set in motion downward by raising the arms sideways and upward. As the board recoils upward because of the arm swing the arms rise further above shoulder height, the heels are raised and the toes press into the board. On no account must the feet leave the board, as this fault is severely penalised. Some divers like to take a deep breath as the arms are raised. There is then a very slight pause with the arms at the top of their movement.

2. *The Crouch*

Now the knees start to bend into a crouch and the arms swing downward and sideways and slightly backward towards the hips. This action will relieve the weight on the board and it will remain still.

3. *The Drive Down*

The board now starts to descend for a second time as the arms, slightly bent, continue their swing vigorously forward and upward past the thighs in time with a strong leg push. This combined arm and leg action co-ordinated with the downward recoil of the board will drive the board down with greater force. When the board reaches its lowest point the hands will be approximately at head level, the knees bent and heels down on the board. There should be no suggestion of backward lean and the shoulders should be directly over the feet.

4. *The Push Up*

As the board recoils pushing the body upward the legs give a strong final push — knees and ankles are extended vigorously, toes thrusting into the board. This combined action co-ordinated with the upward recoil of the board will give the diver maximum height for his flight.

As a land drill the take-off is best taught with arm swing only and then arm swing plus leg movements. A rhythmic command for both on land and on the board may be 'down, up! . . . back, up!'

The angle of take-off should be as near the vertical as possible but very slight modifications are necessary according to the dive. A pike dive, for example, with its very vertical entry has a more vertical take-off than does the swallow dive or a reverse movement. Only an experienced diver can modify his take-off angle to suit the dive he is to perform and still obtain maximum height from the board. The standing take-off can be done *backward* (see pages 66 and 67) as well as forward, with a few alterations:

1. In the stance the heels project over the edge of the board with the weight of the body resting on the balls of the feet and the shoulders should be kept over the edge of the board throughout, even if this necessitates a slightly forward lean. The heels must be level with the board, and on no account should the body be poised on the toes.

2. The take-off is, of course, upward and slightly backward. More care is required here to keep the body and head upright. There is a natural tendency at first to look down at the board.

It is probably best to leave backward take-offs until the pupil has thoroughly mastered the standing and running forward take-offs together with the fundamental jumps. However, the backward take-off may be introduced earlier if the teacher is confident of his pupil's ability and he shows a desire to try something new. Some of the elementary jumps are more easily done backward once the back take-off has been learnt. The back tuck jump is easier to perform than the forward tuck jump as there is less forward momentum from the board and more attention can be paid to the attainment of the tuck position. The sequence of teaching must be left to the teacher, who should have a full understanding of his pupil's needs and desires.

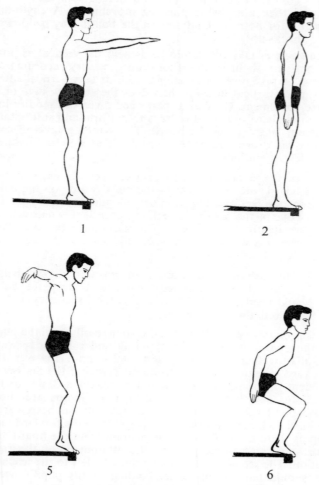

FIG. 7 —STANDING SPRINGBOARD TAKE OFF

3

4

7

9

The approach

The teacher should be aware of the necessity for a good approach from the very beginning of springboard work, if the diver is to acquire the habit of a good controlled approach. The beginner should not be unduly worried with it until definite practice of the simple dives begins.

The approach does not count in the judgement of a dive but it does leave an impression with a judge no matter how hard he may try to avoid this. More important a good approach prepares the diver for the dive ahead. It gives him confidence and enables him to reach the end of the board without unduly oscillating it.

The diver should stand erect at the back of the board and concentrate on the dive to be performed. Once the mental picture is clear he should walk forward confidently, head up, and arms swinging naturally, with equal paced steps. Eyes should look at the end of the board without lowering the head. The position for the stance should be taken up without undue shuffling and movement of the feet. On no account should the diver fumble and feel for the end of the board, afraid to look down.

With the backward take-off there is a *pivot step* to turn the back to the water. At the last step the forward foot should stop momentarily about three inches from the end of the board with the body weight on the rear foot. The body is then turned briskly around on the heel of the forward foot with the rear leg simultaneously swung round straight to join the forward one. The arms may be swung round from the shoulder to assist in the turn. An ordinary about turn may be substituted for this pivot step but this calls for a more accurate and lengthy stop before the turn.

The approach is exactly the same in firmboard work. It requires practice and is an essential part of a diver's repertoire.

BOARD BOUNCING

Board Bouncing was a very common practice with the older type of springboards. With the advent of more flexible boards this is no longer a necessary exercise and indeed it may well affect the life of the springboard. It was used primarily as a warming up exercise before diving, and secondly as a method by which the diver could accustom himself to the board. Modern boards are clearly marked with their degree of flexibility and the diver knows immediately the amount of recoil he may expect the board to give. If, indeed, any time is to be spent in mastering a new or unaccustomed springboard then it ought to be spent in practice of actual take-offs and dives. In other words a correct run up approach or hurdle step followed by a dive or jump.

Again, with the standing take-off the same procedure should be followed. Divers in competition still use a modified form of a single bounce to obtain the feel of the board. This is probably a nervous reaction rather than a worthwhile practice — something which relieves the tension within the diver before he goes to do his actual competition dive.

Board Bouncing is extremely wasteful too, when a whole group has to stand back and watch someone using a board continuously for 2 or 3 minutes in which time perhaps five or six dives could be performed.If warming up is required before actual diving commences, land exercises are much to be preferred.

THE RUNNING TAKE-OFF

The take-off is composed of 5 sections each running smoothly into one another. (See plates, page 65).

1. The Stance

The diver assumes the position of attention, a measured distance from the end of the springboard. This distance, the length of his run-up, the diver can pace out immediately before his dive if he is uncertain. The eyes are on the end of the board without lowering the head. The diver is concentrating on the dive to be performed. This is essential. It prepares the diver mentally and makes him oblivious to the noise and movement of the audience. This very concentration during a competition draws the attention of the crowd to him.

2. The Walk

Without the hurdle step the walk consists of a minimum of 3 paces. The first 2 steps are normal walking steps but the third should be slightly longer and faster showing a gradual acceleration and gathering of effort. The walk is smooth and even and is really a heel and toe glide. The heel meets the board first in order not to oscillate it unduly. The speed and the length of each pace of the run gradually increases. The arms are relaxed at the sides or else swung forward and backward together in line with the run. This swing must never be exaggerated, and it must be co-ordinated with the movement of the legs. The swing is so arranged that the arms are slightly behind the hips at tne end of the run. The eyes should be focused on the end of the board throughout.

3. The hurdle step

This occurs 2 to $2\frac{1}{2}$ feet from the end of the board, that is less than one normal walking pace. In recent years, however, a longer and bolder hurdle step has been used, particularly by American divers, and it certainly lessens the tendency for back lean on the hurdle. As the last step of the run is taken the arms are swung from behind the hips, forward and upward and almost touching as they pass in front of the face, and then opening out above the head to form an angle of about 45 degrees. Meanwhile the rear leg is carried forward and upward as the body springs upward from the forward foot. The rear leg is bent at the knee in its upward movement until the highest point of the spring or hurdle is reached, when it is stretched downward alongside the forward leg. Legs and body are stretched straight down towards the end of the board on which point the eyes are still focused, entailing now a slight downward bend of the head. Toes are pointed.

4. The Crouch

As the body descends the arms are carried outward, downward and inward to the hips, care being taken to see they never pass too far behind the body. This arm movement should be postponed until the legs have come together; indeed, at the highest point of the hurdle the body seems to 'hang' momentarily. As the hands reach the thighs, the body alights on the board on the balls of the feet.

5. The Drive Down

As the board descends the arms, slightly bent at the elbows, swing vigorously forward and upward past the hips in time with the start of a vigorous extension of the knees and ankles, pushing hard on to the board. This combined arm and leg action, together with a downward move of the board, will drive the board down even further. When the board reaches its lowest point the hands will be approximately at head level with knees still bent and the heels down. The body should be balanced on the end of the board with the shoulders directly above the feet.

6. The Push Up

As the board recoils, accelerating the body upward, the legs give a final strong push, straightening at knees and ankles with the toes thrusting into the board. It is most important to give the last bit of leg drive to the take-off and a final extension of the ankles through to the tips of the toes is very necessary. The body should be as straight and taut as possible at take-off. Slack hinges at ankles, knees, hips, spine and neck mean a buffered take-off and a waste of what the board has to give.

The entire running take-off must be continuous and without hesitation. The lean from the board on take-off must not exceed 10 degrees and is largely controlled by the amount the head is raised after the feet contact the board at the end of the hurdle step. This angle of take-off differs with the dive to be performed. The head moves into the line of flight wanted for the dive.

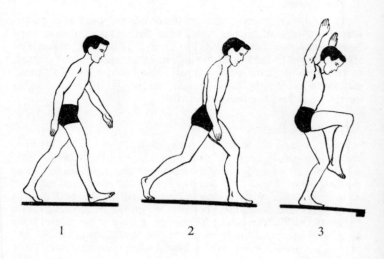

1   2   3

6   7

Fig. 8 — Running Springboard Take-off

The higher the hurdle step the greater will be the resultant depression of the board and therefore the greater its propelling power upward. This height in the hurdle is all important, but it must not be done at the expense of control and balance. Some coaches use a long pole or cane over which the pupil has to leap in his hurdle. This practice may be useful to increase the height obtained by an experienced diver but with a beginner it may well tend to upset him and lead to the pole being cleared at all cost without regard for the execution of the movement.

The running take-off is best practised on land first, in the following order:

1. The stance and run (three paces, others can be added later when the diver is more experienced).
2. The lift forward of the rear leg and knee added.
3. The arm swing for the run and the hurdle.
4. The run with lift of the rear leg now transformed into the spring of the hurdle, together with the arm movements.
5. The final leap-off.
6. The complete take-off to the command 1, 2, 3, Up! and Down! Up!

Once the rhythm of this movement is established it should be practised in a marked space equal in size to the springboard. Practice on the actual springboard should start when the pupil can confidently land on the end of his marked out 'board' consistently.

Actual board practice should be done with a plain jump forward and later with a plain header forward to accustom the pupil to a different line of flight and hence a different angle of take-off.

It is almost impossible to spend too much time in perfecting the springboard take-offs. Sixty per cent of all diving faults originate in the take-off. No diver, however experienced, can afford to neglect practice of these skills. This stage of diving teaching must be well learnt and never forgotten!

CHAPTER IV

HIGH BOARD DIVING

THE ESSENTIAL difference between diving from a springboard and from a firmboard, as in High Board Diving, is that no height is obtained from the latter board. The take-off from the firmboard should be upward but rather more outward than from a springboard and work on the firmboard should not commence until some springboard diving has been experienced.

Competitive High Board Diving is divided into 6 groups, the first 5 of which coincide with those of the springboard, whilst the sixth consists of dives which commence with an armstand balance. For the first 5 groups the diver should learn his dives in the first place from a springboard and then, after mastering the firmboard take-offs, take these dives on to the firmboard. However, where facilities for springboard diving are not available, beginners may be encouraged to take part in firmboard diving if this is the only possibility open to them. Remember, however, that once a week on the springboard is worth ten times that much practice on a firmboard if one has regard to pure diving technique.

Standing Take-off

The stance

Take up an erect position at the edge of the board with the toes overlapping and lightly gripping the edge. The body should be erect, head up, chin in, chest out, legs together, the arms straight and close to the sides with the fingers slightly curled from the second joint. The heels should be together but toes may be touching or apart. The body weight should be evenly distributed over the whole of both feet. When the position is *Firm* and *Confident* without any strain, the arms may be raised forward and upward to the same width and level with the shoulders. The arms should be perfectly straight without any bending of the elbows, thumbs and fingers straightened and close together with palms facing downward.

From this optional position, which may be made to assist balance, the arms are lowered to the sides. It is when the arms move from this position that the dive is judged to have commenced. For multiple forward and inward somersaults the arms are raised above the head. This is to assist the rotation of the body by a more vigorous arm movement downward.

The Take-off

From the position with the arms by the sides, the arms are moved back slightly behind the body and then swung forward and upward in front of the body. At the same time the knees bend and then vigorously stretch, finishing with an extension of the ankles. The feet should leave the board as the hands pass the face and the body should quickly assume a fully stretched position, arms, body and legs in one straight line. The take-off should always be bold, upward and very slightly outward.

Practice of the stance and take-off can be done as a land drill and then from the bath side with a plain jump forward. It should then be used with a tuck dive. Care must be taken to see that 'topple' is not introduced into the take-off and that the push up is through the line of the hips.

Back Take-off (see plates, pages 74 and 75)

This is identical with the forward take-off except that the stance is taken up with the back to the water and heels over the edge of the board, as described for the springboard back take-off. The shoulders must be over the feet to obtain a proper balance. For backward dives the take-off begins with the arms by the sides. For inward movements it is more usual to have the arms raised above the head.

The Running Take-off (see plates, pages 74 and 75)

The Stance

The diver takes up a position similar to that for the springboard take-off, standing erect and at least 4 paces from the end of the board.

The Run

This should be smooth, bold and confident. The body should be upright and the arms swung gently parallel to the line of the run although arm movement is at the discretion of the diver. The take-off may be from one or both feet. With reverse movements the 'run' is often a controlled walk.

Two Foot Take-off

This is the most common take-off, certainly the easiest following on from springboard work, and it is used more commonly than any other. Indeed, it is a modification of the springboard take-off. The hurdle step, as it were, is not so high and of course the fact that the board does not 'give' on landing makes the push up from ankles and knees much more important. The take-off is upright and the greatest height of all firmboard take-offs is obtained with it. The speed of the run, whilst much greater than that of the springboard take-off, should be controlled so that the body's forward momentum is reduced to a minimum and the maximum amount of power put into obtaining height.

There are two positions for the arms at the moment the feet land on the board. It is usual to have the arms by the side as in the springboard take-off and to throw them forward and up-ward in time with the leg push. However, to assist in obtaining additional rotation for multiple somersaults, it is possible to land with both arms above the head in order to pull down with the arms, as in the case of the standing take-off, to obtain extra rotation.

One Foot Take-off

This is used generally for reverse movements and is per-formed at a much slower pace than the two foot take-off. Indeed it is virtually a walk along the board. On the last step the arms are swung forward together, followed by a kick for-ward from the rear leg to give a reverse rotation to the diver. It is very important that the front foot in this step should land as near as possible to the end of the board. Once in the air the legs and feet must be brought together immediately. This take-off does not enable the diver to obtain much lift but it does help him to initiate the reverse movement.

Faults to avoid

1. Don't run too slowly. Try and gain sufficient momentum to obtain height in the take-off. But don't run too quickly or lack of control may result.
2. Don't pause or hesitate during the run. See that your paces are even and smooth.
3. Don't bend forward from hips or neck. Keep the body straight without strain.
4. Don't run straight off the board. You must obtain height from the board to do a good dive. The higher you get, the more time you have to execute your movements.
5. Don't wave or swing the arms unduly.

Armstand Dives

Before attempting any dives in this group it is essential that the diver should be able to perform an armstand balance in the gymnasium with ease and confidence. This is most important, as the steadiness of the armstand balance is judged in these dives. Furthermore, it is quite dangerous to attempt armstands from a high board if the diver is at all uncertain.

Starting Position

The diver should take a position about two feet from the end of the board facing the water with the body erect, arms straight and close to the sides. He should then bend forward, placing his hands on the end of the board, a little more than shoulder width apart, and with the fingers gripping the front edge.

Take-off

The diver should then throw or press up into a straight arm balance. It is easier for the beginner to do a throw up but the results of this may be disastrous if control is lacking. A diver using this technique may easily kick too hard and go straight over into the water. It is preferable to do a press up by

3. HURDLE STEP

2. WALK

1. STANCE

6. PUSH UP

5. DRIVE DOWN

4. DESCENT INTO CROUCH

RUNNING SPRINGBOARD TAKE-OFF (See text, page 55)

6. MOMENT OF
TAKE-OFF

5. PUSH UP

4. CROUCH

4 — OPENING OUT — 3

3. PREPARATORY ARM SWING   2. STARTING POSITION   1. OPTIONAL STANCE

BACK SPRINGBOARD TAKE-OFF (See text, page 51)

2. PEAK OF FLIGHT   1. TAKE-OFF

FORWARD DIVE PIKED (See text, page 86)

5. ENTRY

4. PREPARING FOR ENTRY

4. OPENING OUT

3. PEAK OF FLIGHT

3. OPENING OUT   2. PEAK OF FLIGHT   1. MOMENT OF TAKE-OFF

FORWARD DIVE WITH TUCK (See text, page 86)

2. APPROACHING PEAK OF FLIGHT   1. MOMENT OF TAKE-OFF

REVERSE DIVE PIKED (See text, page 91)

6. ENTRY

5. OPENING OUT

4. BEGINNING TO
OPEN OUT

3. OPENING OUT

3. PEAK OF FLIGHT   2. APPROACHING   1. JUST AFTER
                          PEAK   TAKE-OFF

BACK DIVE PIKED (See text, page 89)

2. PEAK OF FLIGHT   1. JUST AFTER TAKE-OFF

INWARD DIVE PIKED (See text, page 94)

1. TAKE OFF

2. SIDE ARCH

5. LEGS BEGINNING TO TURN

6. PREPARING FOR ENTRY

FORWARD DIVE ONE TWIST STRAIGHT (see text, page 94)

3. ROLLING OVER

4. UPPER TRUNK TWISTED
   LOWER BODY STILL STRAIGHT

7 — ENTRY — 8

FORWARD DIVE ONE TWIST STRAIGHT (see text, page, 94)

1   LANDING   2.   JUST AFTER TAKE-OFF

FIRMBOARD RUNNING TAKE-OFF (See text, page 62)

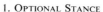

1. OPTIONAL STANCE   2. STARTING POSITION

FIRMBOARD BACK TAKE-OFF (see text, page 62)

3. HEIGHT OBTAINED

3. ARM SWING

4. JUST AFTER TAKE-OFF

1. STARTING POSITION

2. BEGINNING TO LEVER UP

5. CONTINUING TO OVER-BALANCE

6. PUSHING FROM THE BOARD

ARMSTAND SOMERSAULT PIKED (see text, page 79

3. BALANCE

4. BEGINNING THE TAKE-OFF

7. "SITTING" INTO THE PIKE

8. PREPARING FOR ENTRY

ARMSTAND SOMERSAULT PIKED (see text, page 97)

1. Balance   2. "Cutting Through"

Armstand Forward Cut Through with Tuck (see text, page 97)

TRANSFER MOMENTUM IN TWIST DIVES
(note the twisting against the board just before take-off)
(see text, page 94)

FORWARD DIVE STRAIGHT, ELIZABETH FERRIS

(see text, page 121)

bending the legs, knees and ankles, pushing up the hips and then gradually extending the legs until a steady vertical balance in the straight position is achieved. It must be remembered that an excessively hollow back looks most ungainly and should be avoided at all costs. When this steady balance has been achieved the head is dropped between the arms to initiate the forward rotation and the hands push vigorously against the board to clear it and in fact to gain a little height. Remember that the take-off is judged to have commenced when both feet have left the board.

PROGRESSION

How should firmboard diving be commenced? Ideally it should begin with the practice of the standing forward take-off from the 5 metre board or even less if such a firmboard is available. This standing take-off should be mastered first with a plain jump and then with a plain header. The next stage is to try this take-off backward with an inward tuck to begin with and then a back dive with pike. It is essential that these movements should have been learned already on the springboard. Next must come practice on the running two foot take-off. This should commence from the bath side and then be taken up on the 5 metre board and performed initially with a plain jump and then later with the plain header. As with learning the springboard take-off, no undue stress should be placed on the technique of the dive or jump; concentrate instead on the take-off. The reverse movement can be practised from a single footed take-off with perhaps a reverse somersault or reverse dive straight at first, and this can well be performed from a lower board than 5 metres if so desired.

Armstand dives should commence on bath side with an armstand dive straight in order to make certain that the balance is correct. The next armstand dive to master is the armstand dive with forward cut through which involves a different type of take-off. In this case the hips and legs have to swing between the arms for entry, but more reference to this is made in the chapter on key dives.

C

CHAPTER V

KEY DIVES

THE PRELIMINARY jumps and the key dives are the framework upon which all further diving is built. The jumps teach balance and the basic positions used in diving. The key dives embody the fundamental principles required in each group of dives.

The plain jump

Before commencing springboard diving the plain jump has to be mastered as part of the practice for the take-offs. This affords the easiest method of entering the water. However, it must be remembered that the jump has no value in competitive diving and by virtue of the straight position held throughout, the take-off is at its simplest with little or no lean and an almost vertical take-off. It was customary to include a whole series of jumps in the basic positions. These have lost favour with most coaches because the divers practise an angle of take-off which they will never use in competition. The plain jump, however, must be learned in order that a diver may concentrate upon the technique of the take-off.

As the body leaves the board, from the springboard take-off, either running or standing, the arms should continue their swing forward and upward until they are straight above the head and the whole body vertical. Care should be taken not to force the legs back, causing hollowing of the back. As the body descends from the peak of flight, the arms are lowered forward and downward to the sides, with the hands placed firmly against the sides of the body or on the front of the thighs. This position is held as the body enters the water, feet first with toes pointed. The entry should be between 2 and 3 feet in front of the end of the board. On no account must the arms be bent, forming what is commonly called 'jug handles'. The head must be kept up throughout with eyes on a distant point in front of the board. The body must be perfectly straight the whole time, with the shoulders parallel to the edge of the board

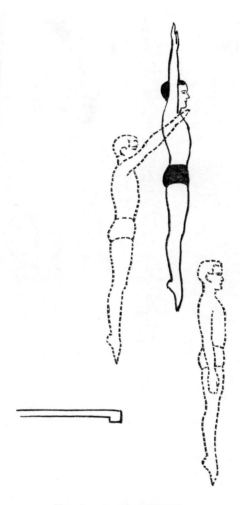

FIG. 9 — PLAIN JUMP FORWARD

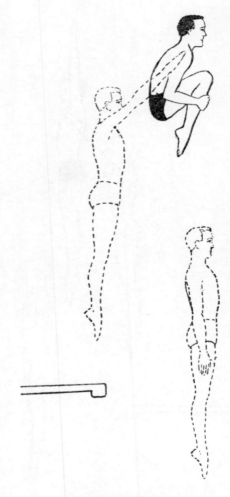

FIG. 10 — TUCK JUMP

With beginners it is useful to add to this jump, a tuck position during flight as a variety and as an exercise in control, but it ought not to be pursued as a definite diving movement. In this **tuck jump,** just before the peak of the flight the knees are brought up to the chest, with the knees and ankles kept together. The toes are pointed whilst the hands grasp the shins and pull them tightly into the body. The trunk is bent slightly forward but the head is kept up. As the diver descends the body is vigorously straightened out for entry as in the the plain jump. Again, it is most important to keep the head up and eyes focused on a distant point.

KEY DIVES

Once the take-offs have been mastered with the use of the two jumps previously described, the diver can begin to consider the key dives. There are 5 groups of springboard dives and a further one for highboard diving and for each there is a basic dive, with two in the case of armstand group from the firmboard. They contain the basic elements of all the remaining dives in that group. This Basic or Key Dive in each group may not necessarily be the easiest dive to perform, but it is certainly the one which every diver should attempt to learn thoroughly first, so that he is then competent to go on to the remaining dives in that group. It may be that in the reverse group, for example, where the reverse dive pike is a key dive, he will find it easier to begin by performing a reverse dive straight. After the elements of reverse take-offs have been mastered, the diver should certainly proceed as rapidly as possible to the reverse dive pike and ignore the previous attempts at the reverse dive straight for competition purposes.

In order to assist the beginner there are appended also the descriptions of preliminary dives and basic movements leading up to the key dives.

Forward Dives

The key dive for this group is the forward dive piked, but most probably first practices will begin with the forward dive with tuck.

Forward dive with tuck (see plates, pages 69 and 68)

As the feet leave the board from the springboard take-off, the head should be kept up as the hips rise and the knees are brought up in front of the body into a tuck position. As the top of the flight is reached the shoulders are dropped forward as the body begins to turn. The diver, as he begins to fall head first, should open out by stretching the legs in line with the body, raising the shoulders and straightening the arms beyond the head for the entry position. This position he should maintain until his entry into the water is complete. Care should be taken to see that the tuck is as tight as possible, but on no account should the head come down on to the chest during take-off, or somersaulting may well ensue. Once this dive has been mastered and the diver has the idea of forming a shape in the air and opening out for entry, the forward dive pike can be attempted.

Forward dive piked (see plates, pages 67 and 66)

This is commonly known as a 'jack-knife' and is perhaps the first 'fancy dive' youngsters attempt if left to their own devices. The angle of take-off is very vertical indeed and the body is projected upward with very little forward momentum. The diver should feel as if there were a hook attached to his lower back lifting his hips up to the ceiling. As the body rises from the board, it bends slowly at first from the hips into the pike position but the head is kept up. The feet move forward slightly to a position in front of the hips as the hands reach down to touch the toes. In the earlier stages the diver should be allowed to touch his shins so that he is not unduly worried about the position in the air. The pike position must be clearly shown and held until the body begins to descend. The legs are then lifted slowly behind and upward until the entry position is achieved. This move must be controlled and the legs firmly checked at the vertical. The arms will be stretched beyond the head which is dropped forward into the absolutely vertical entry position. The commonest fault with this dive is to begin to pike too soon. The emphasis throughout should be on the hip lift.

First attempts can be made from the side of the bath and then

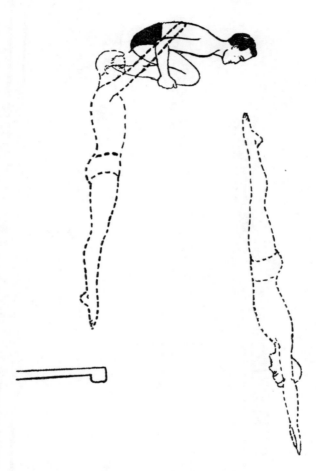

Fig. 11 — Forward Dive with Tuck

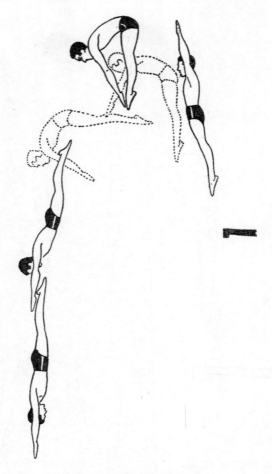

Fig. 12 — The Forward Dive Piked

standing on the springboard, but work should soon begin on running movements because these are what will count in ultimate competition.

Back dive piked (see plates, pages 71 and 70)

Before attempting the back dive piked it is essential that the diver should have experienced the back springboard take-off with a plain jump. Following this, when the mechanics of the take-off have been truly established, practice in back dives should commence. Work should begin from the side of the bath. Here the diver should take up a crouch position on the edge of the bath, back to the water, heels projecting over the edge. The arms should be raised forward in line with the shoulders. From this position he can push vigorously upward and outward, swinging the arms back beyond the head, and by moving the head and shoulders back just before the feet leave the bath side, obtain a curved flight through the air and a head-first entry into the water. In case of any initial fear on the part of the performer, a stander-by can kneel on the bath side by the side of the diver to give support, if necessary, by firmly pushing with his arm under the lower legs if the diver appears to be falling short or if his feet fall back on to the side of the bath.

Once the idea of this backward entry is firmly established, the back dive straight can be attempted from the side of the bath. Here the diver takes up the normal back stance position with the arms stretched out in front of him, in line with the shoulders. He should overbalance ever so slightly as, bending knees and ankles, he pushes vigorously upward and outward, head and shoulders moving back for a head-first entry. From the side of the bath this may well go a little short at first and the diver will have to be encouraged to push up more strongly.

The next stage will be to attempt this from the 1 metre springboard with the springboard standing take-off. Take-off is exactly the same as that with which he performed the back jump from the springboard, except there is a little more emphasis on the upward arm swing and the head and shoulders move backward just before the feet leave the board, in order to obtain the necessary backward rotation. At the top of the flight the arms should be closed and the head dropped backward until the water is visible. The head then returns to its normal position between the arms. The body, almost straight, descends into the entry position, fully stretched with the toes pointed throughout. Once this has been perfected the arm movement of the back dive straight can be added. As the head moves backward the arms are moved outward into line with the shoulders and are kept firmly pressed back. As soon as the diver sees the water the arms should be brought together again beyond the head for the entry position. This is the back dive straight; now the pike position must be added to it.

The first stage is to go back again to the bath side and to practise pike drops into the water. The position is taken up as previously, with the diver standing erect, back to the water, heels just over the edge, arms raised forward in line with the shoulders. From this position he pushes strongly upward and outward and brings his arms forward to reach for his toes. He holds this position and hits the water first with his buttocks. The head is kept up throughout and care should be taken not to induce unnecessary rotation.

From the small height of the bath side this movement can be performed perfectly safely and accustoms the diver to achieving a pike position.

Back to the springboard and the back dive piked should now be attempted. From the back take-off, the hips should be pushed back beyond the edge of the board as the shoulders are kept vertically above the feet. As the feet give their final push the abdomen is drawn in and the shoulders move back to a position above the hips, setting the body overbalancing upward and outward with backward rotation. The moving of the shoulders backward will enable momentum to be stored in the upper trunk, which will be later transferred to the whole body to provide additional backward rotation when the feet leave the board.

The head is held erect and the arms reach up above the head. Care should be taken to keep this movement smooth, slow and on no account should the arms be jerked back, as this could result in too much rotation being imparted to the body. As the stretched body rises from the board the body begins to bend at the hips, the legs rise up and the arms reach down to touch the toes, or, in the early stages, the shins. The head is kept up until the peak of the flight. The body is now rotating much faster because of the pike position and as it begins to descend the body opens out or unpikes into the straight position. Now the legs remain in line with the flight curve, while the trunk moves back until it is in line with the legs. The stretched body is now rotating very slowly and it should meet the water, hands first, a little short of the vertical and pass into the water in a very steep curve. This curve should be maintained until the feet have disappeared beneath the water. The toes must be pointed throughout and particularly on entry.

Reverse dive piked (see plates, pages 69 and 68)

Reverse dives are really back dives with a forward take-off and it is essential that the back dive should be mastered first before this dive is attempted. Because the diver gains distance from the board in a forward direction, it is also known as a 'half gainer pike'.

Once again preliminary practices can commence from the side of the bath where, standing with one foot forward, toes gripping the edge of the bath, the diver can 'throw' his rear leg forward, push up with the forward leg and so initiate a reverse rotation. The shoulders push upward and the head goes back, and even from the side of the bath a reverse dive can be obtained with practice. At first the pupils will push much farther out from the side of the bath than is required and of course 'short' entries result from such a low height. 'Short' entries should be accepted; the idea to impress on the pupils is to kick up in front of them and to let the head and shoulders go back.

The next stage is to attempt the reverse dive straight standing from the springboard, with the same kick take-off, to accustom the diver to the increase in height and to the recoil of the springboard. Having attempted this it is far better to go into the reverse dive straight from a running take-off than to try it with a normal standing take-off, as the added momentum and height from the running take-off will materially assist a diver in getting into the water in a reasonably correct position. Some divers worry unduly about clearing the board, but if take-off technique has been properly learned and if they are always sure of where their feet are to land on the board, there is no cause for worry. Any undue apprehension about this dive really stems from uncertainty in take-off and this is what requires further training. This reverse movement should not be pursued too strongly because it is the reverse dive pike that is ultimately required. It is sufficient to get the diver into the water head first from a reverse take-off; there should be no attempt to labour him with technique. When the feeling of gaining height has been obtained then the reverse dive piked can be attempted.

In this dive, as the springboard recoils upwards during take-off, the hands reach upward and the shoulders are pressed back. The chest is lifted as the feet give their final push and the shoulders should be directly over them, with the upper back arched and the hips a little forward of the feet. The movement of the shoulders backward will enable momentum to be stored in the upper trunk. It will be transferred to the whole body to provide reverse rotation when the body is in flight. As the body leaves the board it should be reasonably straight with chest lifted, shoulders pressed back and the arms stretching out beyond the head. As the legs rise up into a pike position the arms reach down to touch the toes. At the peak of the dive the body begins to open out for entry; once again the legs remain vertical to the water and the body lowered backward towards the water. The arms should go out sideways from the pike position and then come together again beyond the head for an almost vertical entry. The toes should be kept pointed throughout and a good stretch maintained in the entry position.

At first the diver will perform this dive too far from the board and initial correction should be on gaining more height and coming in closer to the board. He will discover that the greater the height obtained the easier it is to perform the dive.

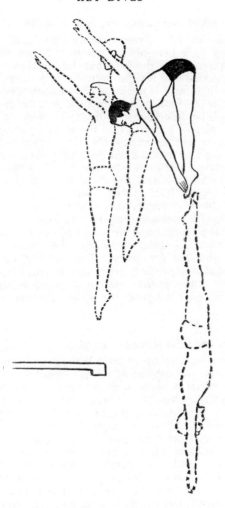

FIG. 13 — INWARD DIVE PIKED

Inward dive piked (see plates, pages 71 and 70)

This is a forward dive from a backward take-off and usually requires very little preliminary practice. It can be attempted standing on the side of the bath but the position for entry can rarely be obtained and it is far better to begin the dive directly from the springboard. If the pupil feels uncomfortable with an inward take-off let him try it in the tuck position first, although there is very little difference in difficulty between the two movements. The take-off requires that the shoulders should remain over the feet for as long as possible. The abdomen is pulled in, the head is kept up as the arms push upward above the head, and the feeling throughout should be of pushing the hips towards the ceiling. Once the diver has left the board, the movements are, in fact, identical with those of the forward dive piked. The body begins to bend at the hips, the arms reach down to touch the toes and the pike position should be reached at the top of the flight and as the body begins to descend the legs are raised upwards and the head drops down between the arms. The diver stretches for entry which should be absolutely vertical, shoulders parallel with the board and with toes pointed. The pike position need not be emphasized at first but for perfection the tighter the pike the better the dive will appear.

Forward dive one twist straight (see plates, pages 72, 73 and 79

By far the largest group of dives is the twist group and here, if a diver wishes to succeed at all in competition, mastery of twisting technique is absolutely essential. It can begin in the initial stages with jumps from the bath side and right from this stage the diver can practise the two fundamental methods of obtaining twist. The first and most obvious method is to take the twist directly from the take-off medium, that is by twisting the body against the feet just before the moment of take-off. This method is used in a variety of ways in the majority of twist dives. In some it plays only a very minor part, and in others, such as the half twist straight, it is normally the only method employed; but the true method of twisting, and by far the most efficient, is to create the twist during flight. This is discussed more fully in the chapter on mechanics of diving. These two different methods of twisting give the coach and teacher a tremendous problem to face when twist dives are commenced. How should twisting be taught to beginners? What method will give the best results?

Unfortunately we are steeped in a tradition of twisting which is made almost entirely by the transfer of momentum method, that is the twist being initiated during the take-off while the feet are still in contact with the board. It would appear that if divers are to succeed fully in the techniques of later multiple twist dives they must, from the very earliest stage, master the reaction method whereby the twist is obtained during the flight by muscular movement.

Undoubtedly both techniques are used instinctively by a majority of divers doing multiple twisting dives, but it would appear equally certain that while the momentum transfer method is essentially natural and requires in fact very little teaching, the reaction method does require instruction and training. Therefore the majority of coaches today are now coming to the conclusion that it is preferable to commence teaching twist dives entirely by the reaction method and to ignore that of momentum transfer. This ensures that from the very beginning the diver is practising the technique that he will require if he is to proceed to really advanced diving.

This, in fact, is the principal reason why the forward dive one twist straight has been chosen as the key dive, because to do this correctly and to obtain precise control over the entry, the reaction technique is the only way of performing this dive.

Preliminary practices again commence on the bath side. The most elementary practice is the half twist push from the side. Here the pupil should stand on the bath edge and bend forward at the waist with the arms stretched beyond the head in a Y position. As the diver pushes off from the bath side, he should press back with one arm and direct the other towards the point of entry, whilst moving the head round with the twist and then centralising it for a backward entry. This elementary twist movement of course is concerned entirely with momentum transfer and serves no more purpose than to introduce beginners to twist movements in the simplest possible way. Once a pupil has gained a realisation of what twisting is, practice should commence from the bath side with the reaction method. This is first done by using the plain jump from the bath side. The diver should be encouraged to get as much spring into the air as is possible, height being the important factor. When confident jumps have been obtained the next stage is to introduce the twisting movement. The best possible method is to allow the pupils to experiment for themselves. Tell them that when they are in the air, at the peak of their jump, they should push their hips round and piking a little, endeavour to turn round in mid-air. Some of the efforts will end in disaster and no doubt with a resounding smack on to the water, but with practice they will find that they can twist as it were against themselves and get round in mid-air. They will discover, with only a little prompting, that to pull round with one arm across the body and push back with the other and to pike even more will assist this rotation. From this point the very elementary twist jump should be taken on to the springboard to fit it into the mechanics of the springboard recoil. The next stage is to attempt the forward dive one twist straight. Let the diver practise one or two plain headers, first getting him to concentrate on more height. The diver should then be encouraged during one of these plain headers to try to turn himself round. He will discover by exploration and by attempting the movements how best he may perform the dive. He will find that he must pike a little, push his hips round and pull round with one arm exactly as he did in the twist jump. He may well in the first few attempts go over on entry. This is no doubt due to too much concentration on the twist and not sufficient on the dive, but at this stage it is immaterial.

The forward dive one twist should be made without any twist taken from the board. It is created during the flight by ensuring that the body is arched either forward, sideways or backward whilst the twist is executed, the twist itself taking place along the spine. The take-off should be square, as for the plain header, and the diver should wait until his feet are in the air before commencing the reaction method. As the body rises square from the board a slight bend at the hips should be maintained and the arms stretched out above the head in a Y position. Assuming the diver is twisting to face left, the left arm should bend slightly at the elbow, pressing back behind the head, while simultaneously the right arm also bends at the elbow and, keeping close to the body, cuts diagonally across the front of the chest under the left armpit, the shoulders twisting quickly to face left. The hips follow the movement, twisting in the same direction as the trunk. The body has now performed a quarter twist and will be in an arch on the right side. The head, which up to that moment was facing the water, now turns quickly to face upward. The left elbow continues to press backward and downward with the left shoulder. The right arm pushes forward and upward, the shoulders twisting upward to the left and the hips following in the same direction. The body should now be in a back arch position, having achieved a half twist. The right arm bent at the elbow is extended in front of the body and the left arm pulled behind in almost a running position. The right elbow and shoulder continue to push diagonally upward across and past the face, as the shoulders perform another quarter twist. The legs are now above the level of the head. As the body is descending for entry, the right arm should now push out above the head and the left arm should follow it for the entry position, both arms moving in this manner to square the trunk for entry by turning the body through the remaining twist, extending one or both arms sideways during this movement.

The arms are brought above the head for the entry which should be parallel to the edge of the board. Care should be taken not to drop the head during take-off or, as previously mentioned, the body would tend to go over on entry, having obtained too much forward rotation.

Armstand Dives (see plates, pages 76, 77 and 78)

In the armstand group of dives there are two key dives, the armstand somersault, which has forward rotation from the armstand and the armstand cut through with tuck, which has backward rotation from the armstand. These two techniques differ entirely from the simple armstand straight. This really is comparable to a jump, as no rotation is taken whatsoever. The diver lifts himself from his hands to clear the board and maintains the armstand position stretched for entry right down into the water. This is an essential dive for beginners, as it can be performed from the bath side and is the easiest way of practising armstand movements in the initial stages, but in the mechanics of take-off it stands in the same relation to armstand movements as jumps do to dives.

The armstand somersault with tuck is the key dive for those armstand movements with forward rotation. The diver obtains a firm armstand on the board and by pressure from his wrist, hand and forearm levers himself from the board, as his chin comes down on to his chest. As he pushes clear of the board he should now be rotating forward, away from the board, tucking up as tightly as possible. As he turns downward towards the water he opens out as soon as he can see his point of entry. The diver pushes his legs out behind him and stretches hard with his arms to the water.

The next dive is the armstand with forward cut through. This can be done in tuck or pike position and from 10 metres in the straight position also, but it is customary to regard the tuck position as the fundamental movement and it is from this position that the more complicated dives are built. Here from a steady balance the diver allows his feet to drop slightly back behind him towards the board as he levers himself from it in his take-off. At the same time he raises his head vigorously and pushes it back. His legs now tuck up and swing through between his arms as they clear the board and he begins to drop to the water. His arms may be raised out sideways from the shoulders or they may be kept by the sides. If the former has been adopted, as soon as the entry is nearing, his arms drop down to his thighs, either by the side or in front, to obtain a stretched and vertical entry. The toes must be pointed throughout. The one danger is to overthrow on the cut through and it is necessary when going up on to the 10 metre board to obtain less backward rotation than that required from 5 metres.

CHAPTER VI

THE MECHANICS OF DIVING

DIVING is basically the art of leaping from a height and entering the water. In doing this the body has first to overcome inertia, that is, the force of gravity acting on its mass and keeping it in the same spot, at rest. A diver standing on a board will remain there forever unless some force is exerted upon him, either from his legs and springing muscles or from someone pushing him from behind. When the force used to overcome the initial inertia is expended the body, now in mid-air, is pulled with ever-increasing speed to the water below by the same force of gravity.

Gravity is the attractive force by which bodies tend to move to the centre of the earth. It pulls bodies towards the earth with a uniform acceleration of 32 feet per second per second. A body falling from rest will travel 16 feet in the first second, 48 in the next and 80 in the third. The total distance fallen in 3 seconds will be 144 feet (16 plus 48 plus 80). The size of the body falling has no effect on its speed. A four-stone weight dropped from a 10-metre diving board simultaneously with a four-ounce weight hits the water below at the same instant. A twelve-stone adult diver falls at the same speed as a boy diver weighing five stones, and takes exactly the same time.

However, this increasing acceleration gives a body greater speed the greater the height from which it falls. As the momentum of the body (which may be regarded as a measure of the impact with which it hits the water) is its mass multiplied by its speed, the higher the dive the harder the body hits the water.

The time of falling can only be influenced by air resistance. A feather has for its weight a very large surface area which, due to friction with the air, slows its fall. If a feather and a steel ball bearing were dropped inside a vacuum tube they would fall at exactly the same rate and take the same time, there being no air inside the tube to slow down the rate of fall of the feather.

Having regard to the comparatively small heights from which diving is performed and to the make-up of the human body, air resistance is negligible.

TIME OF FLIGHT

The time a diver takes in flight depends on:

1. The energy used in take-off.
2. The height of the board.
3. The angle of take-off from the board.

The take-off force used by the diver to overcome his initial inertia is that exerted by the springing muscles in his legs and feet. It is aided in springboard dives by the recoil of the board. Thus, in springboard diving a diver can obtain much greater force for his take-off and hence go higher up from the board than with firmboard diving.

The body moving upward is opposed by the downward pull of gravity which eventually slows the body to a position of momentary rest at the peak of the dive. Then the body begins to fall. The greater the energy used in the take-off, the longer it will take gravity to assert itself and the higher the diver will have reached. Both factors give the diver a longer time of flight. Height from the board is thus all-important in ensuring the diver the maximum time in the air and therefore the maximum time in which to perform the movements of the dive. A good diver is in the air about 1.75 seconds from a 10-metre firmboard and 1.5 seconds from a 3-metre springboard.

THE HEIGHT OF THE BOARD

This must be added to the height obtained in take-off to give the actual height the diver has to fall. With less distance to fall, a diver therefore reaches the water quicker from a 1-metre board than from a 3-metre board and thus a $2\frac{1}{2}$ forward somersault is more difficult from a 1-metre springboard than from the 3-metre board as there is less time in which to com- from the 3-metre board as there is less time in which to complete the movements. Conversely, the higher the board, the more control a diver has to exert, particularly in entry which he makes then with much greater force. Thus, simple dives such as the forward dive and back dive straight are slightly more difficult from higher boards.

ANGLE OF TAKE-OFF

In comparing dives from the same height of board and with the diver using the same energy in take-off, the controlling factor is the *angle of take-off*. Outward movement from the board does not increase the time of flight, only upward movement affects it because the time of flight is directly proportional to the sine of the angle of take-off.

$$T\alpha = Sin. \alpha$$

Where $T =$ Time of flight up from the board and back to the board level.

           $\alpha =$ Angle of take-off measured from the horizontal.

This assumes that the energy used in take-off is constant and as the total energy used in take-off is limited to the strength of the diver and the recoil of the board, energy for outward movement can only be obtained at the expense of energy for upward movement. Thus in practice the further outward the dive, the shorter the time of flight. If it were possible for the maximum height obtained diving from the diving board to remain constant the angle of take-off would not affect the time of flight.

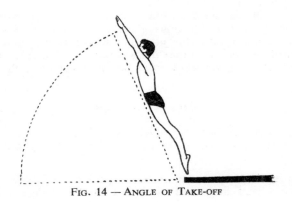

FIG. 14 — ANGLE OF TAKE-OFF

The sines of angles increase the nearer they approach 90 degrees from the horizontal, and the nearer vertical the angle of take-off, the greater the time of flight will be, the energy used in take-off remaining constant.

There must be a slight lean away from the board in the take-off of every dive, otherwise the diver would take off and then land again on the board. Each dive requires a different angle of take-off and small though the differences are, the competent diver must be aware of them. This tendency to forward motion instead of upward may begin in the hurdle step with running dives, the diver beginning to fall forward as he alights on the end of the board before take-off.

Only experience, long training and ardent coaching can assure the diver of control of the angle of take-off. It materially affects the height obtained in take-off and its mastery is the finest art in diving.

Those dives with a very steep line of flight, such as forward dive with pike, require the steepest angle of take-off; those with a flat line, like the forward dive straight, need the flatter take-off. It is most necessary to realize that these differences in angles of take-off are minute, and that height up from the board is the all important factor.

Above all else the diver must realize his outward projection has no bearing on the time of his flight. If a shell was fired from a gun with an absolutely flat trajectory it would strike the earth — even five or six miles hence — at the same time as a shell dropped vertically from the same height as the gun's mouth.

THE LINE OF FLIGHT

The line of flight is the imaginary path traced by a point — the centre of gravity of the body — during its flight through the air.

During flight, the body line or shape is controlled by movements of head, limbs and trunk, but the line of flight remains unaltered no matter what position the body is in. These movements may:

1. Increase the speed of vertical spin — somersaulting,
2. Initiate or increase the speed of lateral spin — twisting,
3. Slow the speed of these spins.

Somersaulting or twisting do not affect the line of flight. In each of these cases the body is rotating about an axis fixed with reference to the body itself. In the case of somersaults the axis is a line through the centre of gravity perpendicular to the plane of the dive, and in the case of the twist is a line through the centre of gravity parallel to the mean length of the body. Similarly the Earth follows a path around the Sun and simultaneously rotates on its own axis.

Flight begins once the feet have left the board and ends when any part of the body touches the water. This is the period when the diver is free from any appreciable external influence other than the force of gravity.

The line of flight is conditioned only by the angle of take-off, the position of the body's centre of gravity at take-off, and the energy of the take-off. Once the board is left, the centre of gravity will follow its predetermined course to the water, no matter what the diver may do. Man, unlike a bird whose wings can push on the air, cannot use any external force to change his line of flight, his air resistance being negligible. The diver can twist or spin around the centre of gravity. He can go in head first or feet first as he wills, but the line of flight moves with inexorable inevitability along its predetermined track. Good take-off is all important for a good dive.

CENTRE OF GRAVITY

The centre of gravity of the body is an imaginary point about which the body balances and is approximately in the centre of the body just above the waist when standing normally erect. In the pike position it is about five inches in front of the body between the abdomen and the thighs. When the arms are raised above the head, the centre of gravity rises in the body to about the height of the fifth rib.

ENTRY

The line of flight should be continued down to the bottom of the bath on entry, so that the entire body passes through the same hole made in the water. The line of entry should be as near 90 degrees to the water surface as possible, but it is not always possible to adjust the line of flight from a curve to a straight line for entry. Jumps, most feet-first entries and the forward pike dive do obtain this absolutely vertical line. In many others, entry is in a steep curve depending very much on the position of the spine. The back dive straight is a typical example, with the back still slightly arched on entry. A vertical or near vertical entry is necessary not only for aesthetic reasons but also because it is the safest position in which the body can take the full impact of entry, and a diver from 10 metres hits the water at approximately 32 m.p.h. A very popular technique for checking lateral turn and speeding up rotation is to re-pike slightly just before entry. This is very often seen in multiple twist dives where, having almost completed the somersault and twist, the diver pikes slightly just before his hands touch the water and then opens up vigorously for a straight entry.

Where the slightly curved entry is obtained, only practice and experience can give the right amount of curve together with good spinal and pelvic mobility. Flight and entry should merge into one, indistinguishable and indivisible.

Entry control is required to correct dives which are going too far over or are too short, as once the body touches the water, muscular action can then be employed to affect the line of entry. These 'saves', although often obvious to a judge will still 'save' valuable points being lost for a faulty entry. They cannot of course make an incorrect dive into a correct one and marks will still be lost. However, the dive will not be as disastrous as if the 'saves' had not been employed at all. The practice of 'saves' has now become a complex art and there are six distinct techniques, all of them giving the appearance of vertical entry by the legs. The body is so moved under the water that the lower legs on entry are kept vertical to the water. A typical one is in a forward dive when the diver is going over badly. As he enters the water he begins to go into a front somersault by spreading his arms out sideways to check the speed of his descent and piking at the waist, to bring his head forward towards the diving board and so keep his legs vertical. This is but one example of this highly technical ability which a first class diver must acquire.

VERTICAL SPIN

All dives are somersaults. Even the simple plain header is half a somersault. They are done in the straight, piked or tucked positions. The diver spins quickest in the tuck and slowest in the straight position. This speed of spin is governed by the law of conservation of angular momentum, which states that, so long as no external force acts on a rotating body, its angular momentum will remain the same. This angular momentum is the product of a body's moment of inertia and its rate of spin.

Angular momentum $=$ Moment of inertia $\times$ Rate of spin.

Should the body's moment of inertia be decreased in some way, e.g., by reducing its radius, the rate of spin must increase in order to maintain the same angular momentum and satisfy the above law. Thus a diver, by drawing up his knees and assuming the tuck position, lessens his body radius and hence his moment of inertia, and therefore spins with a greater angular velocity without any more effort.

In the tuck position the time taken up in somersaulting is less and therefore more time is available for preparing the entry. The body rotates approximately three and a half times as quickly in the tuck position as in the straight. Remember, no matter what is done in the air, the body still falls with the same acceleration. This is why most somersaults are easiest in the tuck position, and why the tariff values of tuck somersaults are usually smaller than for piked or straight ones. This also explains why the open pike position is favoured in many somersaults from the 10-metre board. In the open pike position with the arms held sideways and the head up a little, the body radius is greater than in the closed pike, where the toes are touched or the ankles grasped. When falling from 10 metres, it is often necessary to slow up the speed of spin in order to check more easily when the water is reached, hence the use of the open pike position. Vertical spin in no way affects the line of flight.

The chief factor in a somersault is that for all practical purposes it can only be initiated when the feet are still on the board. A somersault cannot be created in flight nor can it be checked or stopped. A diver creates the illusion of checking a somersault by slowing down his rate of spin, by lengthening the radius of his body around his centre of gravity; e.g., by raising his hands above his head and stretching his body as he comes out of his tuck position. The diver is still rotating until he enters the water and the most perfect timing is required to make this opening out at the correct moment, to achieve what appears to be a vertical entry.

There are four basic methods of obtaining forward angle momentum in dives.

1. Over-balancing or lean.

2. Momentum transfer, which is the transfer of momentum from a part of the body to the whole. For example, in a back dive the arms are swung vigorously upward and backward. When the arms reach the limit of these movements at the shoulder joint, the shoulder will be pulled back and the momentum of the arm swing transferred to the remainder of the body.

3. Eccentric leg thrust. This is when the body is bent slightly at the hips on take-off, so that the push is up through the hip joint causing a turning force to be applied to the body about its centre of gravity. The greater the distance between the hip joint and its centre of gravity, the greater will be the angle momentum created. In other words, the more the degree of pike the greater the somersault momentum.

4. For springboard diving only, eccentric board thrust. This results from the rising springboard thrusting at right angles to its surface. If the body is slightly out of this line this force will pass outside the body's centre of gravity and a turning movement will be imparted. Therefore the greater the amount of lean or hip bend with a springboard dive, the greater this eccentric board thrust will be.

There is nothing in the air a diver can push against to create a somersault. When in the air any movement of any part of the body is accompanied by an *equal* and *opposite* movement of some other part. A diver dropped absolutely vertically from a 10-metre board could bring his arms downwards to touch his toes, and his legs would rise to meet his hands, but this could not create a somersault no matter how long held and the result would be a resounding smack on the water! Somersaults are made during the take-off!

LATERAL SPIN

Lateral spin or twisting can be created in two ways. First of all by momentum transfer which is initiated during the actual take-off. Here the twist takes the form of a continual rotation of the whole body throughout the flight. It is achieved by starting the upper trunk twisting during the take-off whilst the feet are still in contact with the board and usually by turning the shoulders as the feet give their final push. If this twist is done too noticeably the diver would in fact be disqualified under the rules of diving. An anomaly exists that whilst the rules forbid direct twisting from the board, this momentum transfer method has been employed right from the beginning of the twist dives for most of the simple movements. The art has been in concealing it and storing the momentum in the upper body to be transferred later to the whole. The body continues to twist throughout the flight without any further effort on the diver's part.

He can control the rate at which he twists by altering his moment of inertia about his long axis. He will twist more slowly if his arms are stretched out sideways and more quickly if they are by his side or stretched up beyond his head.

The second method of twisting is the reaction method where, by contrary turning movements in the spine and legs, a twist can be created by muscular action during flight. This twist continues only for as long as the muscular action takes place. This is obviously by far the better method of twisting. The diver can control the amount of twist. The twist can be achieved by various methods and often by a combination of several. The easiest way is by using an arm to rotate the trunk; for example, if an out-stretched arm is swung across in front of the body during flight, the body will turn towards it, and this movement can be repeated until the amount of desired twist has been achieved. Secondly, both arms may be used to rotate the hips and legs. If the body is straight and the arms raised sideways then the hips and legs can be rotated by turning the arms and shoulders in the opposite direction to which it is desired to turn the hips and legs. The third method is to use the legs to rotate the upper trunk and this is done by piking, and swinging the legs round in a roughly conical movement. A fourth method is to use the upper trunk to rotate the hips and legs by arching the trunk sideways, forward and backward and twisting it again in the opposite direction to which rotation of the hips and legs is desired. In many twist dives all four or other combinations are used.

The earliest experiments to prove that a diver may twist apparently contrary to physical law were conducted with cats. It was noticed that when a cat was dropped vertically from an upside down position, it twisted and landed feet first. By studying moving pictures it was shown that the cat was able to do this by the flexibility of its spine and by working the rear half of its body with outstretched legs against the forward half in a series of contrary turning movements.

CHAPTER VII

DIVING PROGRESSION

THE SCHEME must be a progressive build-up from fundamental movements and simple dives to the more difficult dives. All dives are elaborations of the elementary plain jump and the plain header. In learning a new dive, practice must be first given to the nearest related simpler dives.

A forward somersault one twist is the product of a full twist dive, and a forward somersault. This complicated dive will never be perfected until its parent dives have been mastered, yet many divers still execute dives without mastering the preliminary movements and wonder why they never improve.

A good coach should have a progressive scheme by which he works, but on no account must he be hard and fast. Work and progression will vary slightly from pupil to pupil, but the scheme must include all the fundamentals of diving. A diver who shows readiness to learn some other dive outside the general scheme should not be restricted provided that the right build up is, or has been, given. A diver should not hammer away indefinitely at an apparent stumbling block at the cost, probably, of his confidence. A change of routine and activity may work wonders and the recalcitrant dive returned to later.

A good scheme should take into consideration future championship conditions, e.g., the Women's 1 metre Championship of England requires 10 dives, two from each group, of which one must be a Key dive or a variant of it and the other, if possible, more advanced. This will tend to give a diver a balanced repertoire. A diver should attempt to have all his competitive dives with head-first entries. They are usually more consistent than feet-first ones, and have greater aesthetic appeal.

PRINCIPLES IN PROGRESSION

The key to progression is *Proceed from the Known to the Unknown*! Build up a new dive from those dives and jumps already known. To this may well be added, *Make Haste Slowly*! A successful build-up is not possible if previous work has been neglected.

The following general principles are worth noting:

1. Most dives are more easily learnt on the 1-metre springboard. The more difficult dives are often easier from the 3-metre springboard due to the greater time in the air in which to perform the movements, but such dives are well outside the province of the learner-diver.
2. Standing dives are usually easier than their running counterparts, but as standing dives must achieve the standard of execution of running ones they are not to be encouraged as competition dives.
3. In somersault dives those in the tuck position are usually the easiest.
4. Never stop practice of fundamentals! A good coach should see every dive a diver knows performed once a week except when in competitive training.
5. Never discourage dives which the pupil has learnt himself but which are outside the general scheme. Such experiments need every encouragement and praise.

A.S.A. TRAINING POLICY

The Amateur Swimming Association recommend that firmboard diving should not be commenced until the diver has reached the A.S.A. Silver Proficiency Standard on the 3-metre springboard.

Springboard diving is the key. Once movements in the air and positions of entry have been thoroughly mastered it is easy to learn firmboard diving which demands only a new take-off. Many American coaches prepare their firmboard pupils by months of springboard work, taking them directly up to the 10-metre firmboard diving only a month before a championship.

The A.S.A. feel that the future of firmboard diving depends on this policy. Two factors have tended to upset it so far — more firmboards than springboards in English swimming baths, and the shortage of first-class firmboard divers (and therefore tempting youngsters to try firmboard work before they are really ready for it).

A diver who masters springboard work first will certainly reap the benefits later. To hurry into firmboard work is to invite trouble. If springboard facilities are only available some distance away, it is worth while to travel there and have even 2 hours springboard practice a week, rather than stay nearer home, and use firmboards.

FIRMBOARD DIVING

Whilst no serious training or competitive work from firmboards should be attempted until the diver has reached the Silver Springboard Standard, 5-metre firmboard work should not be absolutely forbidden to the diver, because it provides a change from springboard work and may well give a little relaxation from intensive training. A coach should not forbid its use, nor should he encourage it.

Once the diver has achieved his Silver Standard, work on firmboards may commence. First let the diver 'feel his feet' on the 5 metre board learning the various take-offs with simple dives. Coach and diver must then decide whether firmboard work is to be practised seriously or not. Many divers do not take to this work because the movements are jerkier in take-off and greater physical strength is required for entry from the higher boards.

If firmboard diving is to be taken up competitively 10 metre work is the aim. The diver should practise on a 7½ metre board before attempting 'the roof' and so become gradually accustomed to the extra control and strength required. This preliminary period should take at least one year, if not two.

For actual competitive training after this preliminary work, dives are best learnt on the 3-metre springboard and only a month of two devoted to intensive practice of 10 metre diving before the competition.

A coach may introduce armstand dives from the 5-metre firmboard long before firmboard work is begun. Armstands are easily learnt by youngsters, and early work in this direction will ease the task later on. Armstands are a good exercise, essential even to the specialised springboard diver. Only the armstand dive straight and the armstand forward cut through should be learnt at this stage. The armstand backward fall, in particular, should be left and included later in specialised firmboard work because unless absolute confidence and control in the armstand is obtained, the diver may go straight over from his balance.

A PROGRESSIVE SCHEME

No scheme can be hard and fast, nor will every coach have the same one, but the scheme used by the author is shown (see end of chapter).

The key to this progression is that no jump or dive is judged satisfactory until it would average 5 marks out of 10 for three consecutive efforts. This does not mean that other movements may not be attempted until the previous one is satisfactory. It may be necessary to begin with an easy dive to establish initial movement and then move more rapidly to the key dive; for example the back dive straight may be learnt before the back dive piked is attempted.

Such attempts can be made but dives containing the as yet not satisfactory movement should not be done. A forward dive piked must be satisfactory before the first attempts at a forward somersault piked. Practice, however, could still be going on at, say, forward dive with tuck, or back dive straight, if their preliminaries were satisfactory. Then comes the forward dive in its three positions. A forward somersault with tuck is introduced early, partly because it is an easy dive for youngsters who somersault naturally, and partly because it is, to most beginners, the first 'fancy' dive, and all learners are anxious and impatient to begin the 'real thing'.

Backward jumps follow as the diver must realise early that forward dives form only a part of the diving build-up. From these jumps the first backward and inward dives are introduced, then the first twist movements.

All the time, the diver should be consolidating the dives already learnt. A forward 1½ somersault can be introduced now that the board confidence and skill have been acquired.

At this stage the diver should be ready for reverse movements. The reverse dive straight should be attempted first but no great efforts made to perfect this, because once the reverse movement has been reasonably established the diver should proceed to the key dive which is the reverse dive piked.

There should now be a period of consolidation with perhaps only one new dive introduced — the inward somersault in order to have at least two dives in each group. In consolidation a diver should learn each dive he has done so far in another position. Whilst perfection may not be necessary in these new attempts they will show where a diver's natural tendencies lie, and will give him more confidence in the original position learnt. Where a diver shows he is better in the new position the coach should have this position perfected and brought up to competitive standard. In most of the dives listed in this scheme, the pike position is usually the easiest to learn next. Once again the international tariff gives the key to progression.

The final stage must include a flying forward somersault C. as an introduction to flying movements. Flying somersaults are now out of favour in competition but they may be useful to some divers who wish for an intermediate stage between a 1½ somersault and a 2½ somersault. Most, however, prefer to attempt a double somersault after a 1½ and then go on to a 2½. Then should come the forward dive one twist straight and the similar dive backward to complete the fundamental twist movements. Lastly the introduction of combination dives, i.e., where a dive is performed and then a twist done before entry, or vice versa. The easiest is the forward somersault half twist.

With this repertoire mastered, the diver is accomplished and ready to learn any other dive. Every other dive contains part of some of the movements learnt already. There can be no rule as to how long it should take to master this repertoire, but two years of consistent practice ought to be sufficient for the would-be champion.

THE INTERNATIONAL TARIFF

This is drawn up by the Federation Internationale de Natation Amateur (F.I.N.A.), the governing body of International Swimming, Diving and Water Polo. This body usually meets at each Olympiad and thus its rules stand for four years at a time without change.

F.I.N.A. decides which dives are permissible in international competition and allocates to each of them a degree of difficulty relative to how simple or hard to perform they are. The degrees range from 1.2 for a forward dive tuck from 1 metre to 3.0 for a forward $1\frac{1}{2}$ somersault Triple Twist, from 3 metre and 2.9 for a $2\frac{1}{2}$ somersault double twist from 10 metre.

By means of these tables a dive can be judged without consideration of the difficulty of the dive to be performed. The judges can see the dive to be judged as a whole; they assess how near it was or was not to perfection. The results of the judges are written down and in National and International contests, the highest and lowest awards are cancelled out and the total of the remaining marks credited to the diver. This is then multiplied by the degree of difficulty to give the diver's score. Thus a diver receives the fullest benefit from attempting more difficult dives.

With five judges, as in a National Championship, J. Brown doing a back somersault C standing from the 3 metre springboard (tariff value 1.5) receives; 5, 4, 5, $5\frac{1}{2}$, 5. The 4 and $5\frac{1}{2}$ are cancelled leaving the diver with 15 marks. This multiplied by 1.5 gives 22.5. The total scores are averaged to one judge at the end of the competition.

The degree of difficulty has a further function in National and International Highboard diving contests where a certain number of dives in each contest have to be performed with a limit on the total of the degrees of difficulty. In the men's highboard events, six dives not exceeding 11.2 in total of the degrees of difficulty must be performed. In this event the divers should choose dives which total 11.2 in order to obtain the maximum benefit.

This may not, of course, always be possible as one dive well done at a lower tariff value than that required may still obtain more points than a higher tariffed dive poorly done.

This selection of a dive or position to give the maximum points also applies to the springboard events, where although the first five dives are specified, the positions are not; and hence a diver may choose the position in which he can do best, rather than one with a higher tariff but which he performs poorly.

Each dive has a code number in the International Tariff which enables competitive diving to be carried out in countries whose language is foreign to the diver. By use of this numbering system the diver can recognise from a number board the dive which he is to perform.

The key is extremely simple. The dives in the first four groups of springboard diving have a three figure coding system. Dives in the twist groups have a four figure system. With the first four groups the first number denotes which group it is. 1 for forward, 2 for back etc., the second figure denotes whether or not it is a flying dive. 0 means non-flying; 1 means flying. The third figure denotes the number of $\frac{1}{2}$ somersaults — 3 indicates that it is $1\frac{1}{2}$ somersaults. The number for a back $1\frac{1}{2}$ somersault is 2 for the group, 0 for non- flying and 3 for the number of somersaults; i.e., 203. In the twist group the first number denotes the group — in this case 5. The second number denotes the allied group from which the dive is taken. There are no flying movements in twist dives so that the third figure denotes the number of $\frac{1}{2}$ somersaults and the final figure the number of $\frac{1}{2}$ lateral turns or twists. Therefore, a reverse $1\frac{1}{2}$ somersault $\frac{1}{2}$ twist reads, 5 for the twist group, 3 for reverse, 3 for the $1\frac{1}{2}$ somersault and 1 for the $\frac{1}{2}$ twist; i.e., 5331.

In the highboard tariff the armstand dives have the first number of 6, an armstand somersault is No. 612, for example.

D*

DIVING PROGRESS CHART

Name ....

Club ....   Date of Birth ....

Commencing ....

At 1 m. No.	Tariff	Dive Name	When first attempted 1 m.	3 m.	When satisfactory 1 m.	3 m.	Coach's Remarks
—	—	Forward plain jump					
—	—	Forward tuck jump					
101	1.2	Forward dive C					
101	1.2	Forward dive B					
101	1.4	Forward dive A					
102	1.4	Forward somersault C					
—	—	Back plain jump					
—	—	Back tuck jump					
201	1.6	Back dive A					
201	1.6	Back dive B					

401	1.3	Inward dive B
—	—	Forward 1 twist jump
5112	2.0	Forward dive 1 twist A
5211	1.6	Back dive ½ twist A
103	1.6	Forward 1½ somersault C
301	1.7	Reverse dive A
301	1.7	Reverse dive B
302	1.6	Reverse somersault C
402	1.7	Inward somersault C
401	1.7	Inward dive A
112	1.5	Flying forward somersault C
5121	1.7	Forward somersault ½ twist D

SATISFACTORY – When 3 consecutive jumps or dives would average 5 marks out of 10.

A.S.A. Bronze Proficiency Passed .... Date.

A.S.A. Silver Springboard Passed ....

A knowledge of the International Tariff is essential to all coaches. It provides a ready-made table of progression within the various groups and is indispensable for competitive work.

A.S.A. PROFICIENCY AWARDS FOR DIVING

These diving tests, of which details are appended at the end of this book, should play their part in a progressive coaching scheme.

They provide ready-made and standardised tests. They provide the coach with the chance of outside and experienced opinion of his pupil's work. Success in the tests is a great boost to a diver's morale, and it provides an incentive for training.

CHAPTER VIII

ESSENTIAL FEATURES AND
THE JUDGING OF DIVING

IT IS not the task of this book to set out the Rules of Diving. These can be found in the A.S.A. Manual on Diving. Given here is the application of these rules to the coach and teacher. There are certain things which just have to be done, and others upon which there is general, if unwritten, agreement and which must be fulfilled if a diver is to be judged satisfactory.

These essential features — written and unwritten — must guide the work of every coach. These are the standards he must measure up to. The assessment of a dive is very similar to that of a painting — it is largely a matter of personal opinion, but the rules and scope are narrower; a surrealist version of a forward somersault would make little impression on the judges of a contest! The coach's ideal dive must be a combination of his own and the accepted ideas of recognised judges of diving.

The rules dealt with here are those governing F.I.N.A. and A.S.A. Championships; local bodies are at liberty to make their own provided they are clear and available to the diver, but local conditions should be kept, wherever possible, within the framework of A.S.A. rules.

TAKE-OFF

Judges are not allowed to consider the approach to the starting position. Nevertheless attention ought to be paid to these points. A smart approach unquestionably creates a favourable first impression in the mind of a judge, just as a poor, careless one will have a reverse effect. Judges are human beings, not machines; they can be impressed. More important though, in the approach, is the effect it has on the diver. With a good controlled approach, the diver can brace himself mentally and physically for the task ahead.

The taking up of the starting position or stance is not judged, but unnecessary movements in obtaining a comfortable position should be avoided. For all standing dives the starting position is when the diver stands erect on the edge of the board, with the arms by the side or above the head. The arm swing is judged to have commenced once the arms leave the starting position. They may be brought up above the head to assist in the beating down (for multiple somersaults for example) or they may be swung up into the dive from position of attention, but the dive commences when the arms move.

In running dives the starting position is when the diver is ready to take the first step of his run. A diver is deemed to have commenced his dive from the moment the starting position is taken up. See the starting position is good. The diver is stationary and most easily judged at this point. It has a great effect on many judges and no diver can neglect practice of it and the good posture it entails.

The run itself must always be smooth, straight, without hesitation, and consist of not less than three steps before the jump to the end of the board. This means at least four steps as the jump is but an exaggerated step. If a dive takes less than four steps the referee deducts 2 points from each judge's award.

The take-off must be bold, reasonably high and confident. In running dives, the take-off from the springboard must be from both feet simultaneously, but from fixed boards the take-off can be from one or both feet. When performing a standing dive, the diver must not bounce on the board before take-off. In a running dive the diver must not stop his run before the end of the board and make more than one jump on the same spot. Standing take-offs for forward movements from the springboard are permissible but they are severely handicapped in that judges are required to award points for a standing dive bearing in·mind the height and standard of execution which might be expected for a running dive.

A diver may not have a trial bounce on the springboard until after the score of the previous diver has been announced.

A diver may restart the take-off of both standing and running dives but the referee would deduct 2 points from each judge's award for this, in a competition. Stopping again on this second attempt would cause the referee to declare it a failed dive.

In armstand dives the diver must show a steady balance with body straight. If this is not shown each judge may deduct from 1 to 3 points. The diver should aim at a balance of at least two seconds.

Should a diver doing an armstand fail to obtain his balance and obtains it in a second attempt, the referee will deduct 2 points from each of the judge's awards. The diver may remove his hands from the board in concentrating for his second attempt. If this attempt is unsuccessful the referee will declare it a failed dive.

FLIGHT

A dive may be done with the body straight, piked or tucked. Most dives may be performed in these three different ways. Some, like the forward $2\frac{1}{2}$ somersault from a springboard may be attempted in only two of these positions. In others, usually the most difficult dives, the choice of the position is left to the diver; the reverse $1\frac{1}{2}$ somersault $\frac{1}{2}$ twist from the 3-metre springboard is an example. Finally there are a few dives, such as the armstand dive, which may only be done with the straight position.

Whatever the position it must be clearly shown.

In the straight position, the body must not bend at either the knees or the hips, the feet must be together and the toes pointed. Fingers may be clenched but it is usual to have them straight and together, and this is certainly more graceful. The trunk may be straight or the back slightly hollowed.

When the body is in the pike position it must be bent at the hips, but the legs must be kept straight at the knees, the toes pointed. This position may be obtained by bending the trunk downward to the legs as in the forward dive piked, by lifting the legs up to the trunk as in the pike jump, or by a combination of both as in the header backward with pike.

In the tuck position, the whole body must be as compact and bunched up as possible with the knees together and the toes pointed. If the knees are open the judges may deduct 1 to 2 points.

In all three positions the placing of the arms is at the discretion of the diver. In flying somersaults the arms should be in either the plain header or swallow position during the 'fly' but the latter position is more usual.

In pike somersaults the hands usually clasp the back of the legs with elbows touching the sides of the body, or the arms are carried out sideways into the swallow position, depending entirely on the tightness or otherwise demanded of the pike position in the dive to be done.

In the tuck position the hands almost invariably clutch the lower legs and pull them in to the body, and so help to obtain a tight tuck.

Despite the legal freedom in the use of the arms in dives, a diver should aim to make arm movements as inconspicuous as possible, and most definitely to control them.

The toes in all positions must be pointed and are a factor no diver can overlook. Judges certainly do not! A diver must achieve good ankle flexion.

The diver must do the dive in the position announced. Should a diver, having stated a dive as being in, say, the straight (A) position, execute the dive in either the tuck or pike position, the judges may only award up to 2 points.

ENTRY

Entry into the water must always be as near vertical as possible and never beyond the vertical. A dive is not necessarily a failed one if the entry angle is beyond the vertical, indeed many judges would not award 0 marks in, say, a feet-first entry, unless some part of the body other than the feet had touched the water first. However, this 'going over' is a heavily penalised fault and a vertical entry is an absolute necessity in a perfect dive.

The entry should never be less steep than 30 degrees from the vertical and 'going in flat' beyond this angle is as severely punished as 'going over'.

In all entries the body must be straight and the toes pointed. In head-first entries the arms must be stretched beyond the head in line with the body with the hands close together. The hands need not be touching but as close together as possible. In feet-first entries the arms must be close to the body with no bend at the elbow. The actual positioning of the arms, whether at front, sides or back is left to the diver but having the hands at the back of the thighs is usually frowned on, as in this position it is very difficult to keep the arms straight and close to the body. If the arms are not in the correct position, as often occurs in twist dives, judges may deduct from 1 to 3 points. If the arms are held beyond the head in a feet-first entry, the highest possible award is $4\frac{1}{2}$ points.

The dive is considered finished as soon as the whole of the body has disappeared below the water. The return to the surface is not judged. Nevertheless an inconspicuous return to the surface and to the side of the bath is advised. No judge relishes a wetting!

Entry is perhaps the most easily judged part of a dive and it always impresses spectators more than any other point. Practice of good entries will repay a diver many times over.

TWIST DIVES

These are the most complicated dives and are firmly legislated for.

Twists must not appear to commence from the board, some height must be gained first. It is very simple to twist directly from the board with the assistance of an uneven push from the feet, hence this rule.

D**

A twist should be completed and checked as entry into the water is made.

In all pike dives with twist the twist must not be started until there has been a marked pike position. In all reverse dives with twist, the twist must not be started until there has been a marked header position.

Where the twist is a quarter more or less than desired it is considered a failed dive. Up to this limit a twist is penalised by loss of marks whenever the body and particularly shoulders of the diver are not parallel to the edge of the board on entry.

In somersault dives with twist, the twist may be performed at any time during the dive at the option of the performer.

SOMERSAULTS

Where somersaults with tuck are to be performed (other than flying somersaults) the movements showing the somersault position should be commenced as soon as the feet leave the board. The tuck position is thus taken up during the lift from the board.

In flying somersaults, a distinct and well defined header position must be shown first before the somersault. The somersault must then be done as quickly as possible. The header position should be maintained long enough for the body to have commenced its downward path to the water. In firmboard diving with the flying double somersault the header position may be shown first or between the two somersaults or on both occasions.

THE DIVER

There are a number of rules of which every diver hoping to succeed in competitive work must be aware.

All dives must be chosen from the F.I.N.A. Tariff. One's own inventions are not allowed. But this should not stop any diver from creating an entirely new dive provided it is not used in competition. Should a new dive be generally accepted, there is no doubt it will eventually be recognised by F.I.N.A. and placed in their tariff. Concepts of diving have changed rapidly and it is only recently that twist dives have been performed in competitions from the firmboards.

Dives of the same tariff number are considered the same dive and all voluntary dives must be different. Thus no one may do a forward dive piked and then a forward dive with tuck in a competition. They are the same dive possessing the same tariff number 101, and differing only in the position in which the dive is executed.

Dives performed with a limit to their tariff value may not be repeated as dives without a tariff limit (see Chapter VII).

If a diver executes a dive other than that announced, the dive must be awarded 0 points, if the referee is certain the diver had obviously done this; in doubt he may leave this decision to the individual judges. If the referee has erroneously announced the dive, the diver should correct this announcement at once. but if the dive has been executed, the diver may appeal to the referee who can have such a dive cancelled and the correct one performed immediately.

A dive must not be executed until the referee has given a signal, usually a whistle blast. Should a competitor dive before the signal the referee decides whether or not the dive should be repeated.

If the execution of a dive is adversely influenced by exceptional circumstances, the diver may appeal to the referee immediately after this dive. If the referee considers the circumstances beyond the control of the diver he may allow the spoilt dive to be repeated.

JUDGING

The coach and teacher must have some knowledge and ability in this exacting art. Knowing the rules is not sufficient; practice in the assessment of dives is very important and the greater the experience the teacher possesses of this the better his opinion will be.

The assessment of a dive depends upon what you consider to be the perfect example. Only by seeing the best divers in action can this picture of perfection be maintained and even improved.

The chief attribute judge and coach must acquire is a photographic mind; the ability to see again in his mind the dive which has just been performed. He has not long in which to note all the good and bad points.

The coach requires judging ability to assess the work of his pupils and to decide which dives the pupils should attempt in competitions.

The teacher is often called upon to judge, particularly in competitions with the plain header as the chief or sole dive. Here the teacher is again recommended to see his standard of perfection as the only suitable yardstick. It is fatal to give the first competitor 5 marks and then the rest marks more or less than 5 on how much they were or were not better than the first pupil.

Where the standard of competition is very low some teachers judge out of 20, unknown to competitors and spectators in order not to discourage young triers with twos and threes, but they must be certain no one would reach more than half marks.

All in all it is far better to mark every competition on championship standards. All the judges know what they are attempting to do and it gives the competitors a real standard to measure up to. A boy who wins the 100 yards swimming race in 80 seconds knows he has 30 seconds to remove before he becomes a world champion. The lad who receives 2 for each of his swallow dives knows he must average at least 6 before he can aspire to a championship.

CHAPTER IX

EXERCISES FOR DIVERS

A FIRST-CLASS diver must be a first-class gymnast. He must have:

1. Exceptional suppleness of body — an almost 'rubber' frame.
2. Strength to obtain a good spring and to maintain the entry position.
3. A very good sense of balance.
4. A quick co-ordination of mind and muscle.
5. All-round physical well-being.

To help in the achieving of these objectives, daily exercise is necessary. Ten minutes every day is sufficient for a beginning, but it must be *Regular Every Day*! This period of exercise is best taken after the morning's ablutions, in front of an open window or in the open air. Suitable exercises are many, but it is necessary to have a sequence of exercises in each daily period and progression over a series of periods.

1. *Warming-up* — preparing the body for exercise or work to be done.
2. *Strengthening* — strength to obtain a good spring and to maintain the entry position.
3. *Suppling* — increasing the range of movement of joints, tendons and muscles.
4. *Co-ordination and balance* — improving the control of mind over muscle.

All these classifications may be found in any one exercise but the *main* aim of the exercise should always be clear, e.g., a good warming-up exercise is running on the spot, but it also has a secondary strengthening effect on the legs and ankles.

Besides these general classifications, exercises may be further sub-divided under their immediate aims, i.e., what actual factor in diving they are to improve, e.g., 'forward rools', whilst being, in general, co-ordination exercises, are used in particular to help obtain a good tuck position.

To obtain the maximum benefit from any exercise the diver must know why he is doing it and what part of his diving it will help. The exercise period must be related to actual diving.

Set out in this chapter are three specimen ten-minute tables of exercises. They are designed primarily for indoor individual use, in the bedroom not the gymnasium, but they can also be done by classes. In a gymnasium the scope and range of the exercises can be greatly extended. They are chiefly for the less advanced divers and those aspiring to championship level. The Olympic diver requires a very specialised and intensive course in a gymnasium adapted to his particular needs.

Once a diver has become proficient in an exercise he should proceed to another one with a similar aim but a little more strenuous or difficult, otherwise he will become stale and bored. There can be no hard and fast rule as to how many times an exercise should be done or how long continued. This will depend on the individual, but on no account must he over-tire or strain himself. The exercise period should leave a sensation of well-being and a capacity for further work. The diver must concentrate on each exercise he does. A half-hearted effort is perhaps worse than none at all. To be a success as a diver really hard work is required! Physical fitness is an absolute essential.

BEGINNER'S TABLE

Type	Exercise
Warming-up	Running on the spot.
Neck and head	(Standing feet astride), head dropped forward, chin on chest, then raised slowly upwards, chin in. 'Relax and raise'.
Arm and shoulder	(Standing feet astride), arm across bend, shoulder height, fists clenched, elbow circling backward, change to forward.
Pike	(Standing feet astride), pick up 20 matchsticks from floor, keeping knees straight.

FIG. 15 – WARMING UP – NECK AND HEAD – ARM AND SHOULDER – PIKE

FIG. 16 – TUCK	TWIST	BALANCE

Straight or swallow   Lying on back, arms sideways in line with shoulders, palms on floor, chest raising, keeping back of head on floor.

Tuck   (Standing feet together), hug alternate knee to chest. Head up, back straight.

Twist   (Standing feet astride), arms across bend, trunk turning (from hips) with arm flinging sideways (head looks along flinging arm).

Balance   Marching on toes along a line. Arms may be raised to help balance. Turn on toes and repeat at end of line.

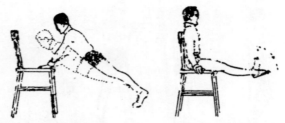

FIG. 17 – STRENGTHENING   SUPPLING (ANKLE)

Strengthening	(High front support position, feet on floor, hands on chair seat, place chair against wall to prevent possible slipping), arms bending (elbows outward) and stretching. Body kept in straight line.
Suppling (ankle)	(Sitting on chair), toes pointing and raising, followed by toe and foot circling.
Depletive (breathing)	(Standing astride), deep breathing, arms raising sideways.

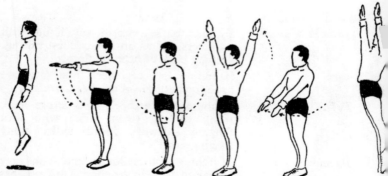

FIG. 18 – SKIP JUMPING   STANDING TAKE-OFF

INTERMEDIATE TABLE

Type	Exercise
Warming-up	Skip-jumping on the spot, followed by springboard standing take-off practice.
Neck and head	(Standing astride), quick head turning to side, chin in.

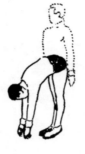

FIG. 19 – ARM AND SHOULDER   PIKE

Arm and shoulder	(Standing astride), 'arms across bend'. Elbows and then straight arms rhythmically pressed backward. 'Elbows and arms!'
Pike	(Standing feet together), floor beating with hands (knees straight), followed by full knee bending rhythmically 'beat and bend and beat and . . .'

FIG. 20 – TUCK

Tuck

(Forward rolls, crouch position with arms outside knees, head dropped forward.) Quick push from ankles, weight of body falls on hands, roll begins with back of head and then back touching the floor Cross legs and stretch to stand up.

Straight

(Head-first entry position. Lying on back, arms above head, palms uppermost, knees bent, soles of feet on floor.) Press lower portion of back against floor; slowly straighten knees until in straight position with toes pointed.

FIG. 21 – TWIST

BALANCE

Twist

(Standing feet astride, 'arms across bend'.) Trunk turning with arm flinging sideways with one press in position. Rhythmically 'left and . . . right and . . . left and . . .'

Balance

Handstanding. Kick up and balance against a wall.

Strengthening

(Front support position on floor), arms bending and stretching (elbows outward, body in straight line).

FIG. 22 – STRENGTHENING

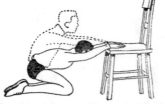

FIG. 23 – SUPPLING (DORSAL SPINE)

Suppling (dorsal spine) — (Kneel sitting. Trunk forward, arms resting at wrists on chair, shoulder width apart). Rhythmical trunk pressing downward.

Depletive — (Posture test standing (stance position) in front of mirror), heels together, knees straight, body erect, shoulders square, head up, arms straight at sides and relaxed.

ADVANCED TABLE

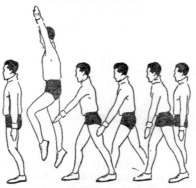

FIG. 24 – SPRINGBOARD RUN AND HURDLE STEP

Type	Exercise
Warming-up	Skip jumping on the spot with rebound. Followed by springboard run and hurdle step practice.

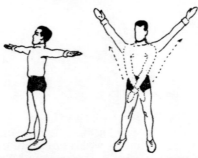

FIG. 25 – NECK AND HEAD   ARMS AND SHOULDERS

Neck and head	(Standing astride, arms raised sideways), palms turning upward with head pressing backward, chin in. 'Press! . . . Relax! . . '
Arms and shoulders	(Standing astride, arms crossed in front of body), both arms flinging to mid-way position with one press in position. 'Up . . . and . . . down, up . . . and . . .'

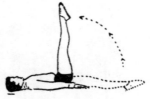

FIG. 26 – PIKE

Pike	(Lying on back), both legs raised to vertical and slowly lowered. Toes pointed, palms of hands on floor.

Straight   (Standing astride, arms downward, trunk
                    forward), alternate arm swing sideways
                    and upward with trunk and head turning.
                    Do not raise trunk, turn from hips, let
                    non-turning arm follow relaxed.

FIG. 27 – BACKWARD ROLL TUCK

Tuck   Backward rolls. Knees full bend position.
                    Body is tipped backward, hands placed
                    on floor beyond shoulders. Rounded
                    back meets floor first and back of head
                    last. Knees bent up to chest until feet
                    touch floor again, when stretch to stand
                    up.

Balance   (Handstanding), kick up and balance
                    without support.

FIG. 28 – STRENGTHENING

Strengthening   (Horizontal front support position. Hands
                    resting on floor, legs on stool level with
                    shoulders). Arms bending and stretching.

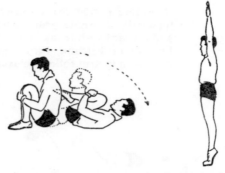

FIG. 29 – SUPPLING   DEPLETIVE

Suppling (spine)   (Sitting and hugging knees tightly to chest), roll backward for head to touch floor and forward to starting position.

Depletive   (Standing feet together), arms above
(entry position)   head, raise on toes and stretch up as high as possible, palms facing front.

PRE-DIVING EXERCISE

Before any diving session is begun, a diver must prepare for the physical demands of diving. He must first 'warm up', preferably whilst clad in a track suit or with a sweater over costume. 'Warming up' exercises should stimulate the blood stream, for a muscle cannot be fully stretched or worked until it is receiving almost the maximum amount of oxygen from the blood. But these exercises should not tire the diver. They must be purposeful and their aims clearly understood.

Some easy examples are: running on the spot; standing astride, both arms circling backward, change to forward.

Then the diver must consider his training programme. If it is to be springboard work he must practise his run up and hurdle step; his standing take-offs, forward and backward, still, of course, in track suit or sweater. Similar practice should precede work on the firmboard.

Before each dive in the training period is attempted, exercises applicable to that dive should be done as follows:

1. An exercise to stimulate the muscles concerned in the fundamental position and prepare them for the work ahead.

2. The sequence of movements to be done in the dive. This will prepare the mind for the split-second control and co-ordination required.

   Examples of these exercises are given on next page.

Forward dive piked

Example 1.   Legs together — vigorous toe touching with hands; knees straight, head kept back, and return to erect position. Repeat 5 or 6 times.

Example 2.   (*a*) Stretch in air as from take-off.

(*b*) Reach down to pike position.

(*c*) Open out into entry position.
Repeat until the sequence of movement is easy and well controlled.

Flying forward somersault with tuck

Example 1.   (*a*) Head pressing backward with arms flinging sideways from standing erect arms by side.

(*b*) Standing erect. Alternate knee hugging to chest, repeat 5 or 6 times.

Example 2.   (*a*) The stretch as for take-off.

(*b*) The swallow position.

(*c*) The tuck (one knee up to chest) with head down.

(*d*) Open out into entry position, arms by sides.

Short periods of exercise can be built up for any dive and should not exceed a minute or two in duration. As they will usually be done between dives, it is best to have a quick rub with a towel first.

FIG. 30 – DIVING EXERCISE FOR A FLYING FORWARD SOMERSAULT

Hand in hand with *Pre-Diving Exercises* must go practice of take-offs when a dive is being learnt, or is not yet perfect. Where take-off practice is done it should follow Exercise 1, and precede Exercise 2.

GENERAL PHYSICAL CONDITIONING

Apart from exercises related to diving there are many other aids to a good physical condition. Some are common-sense, everyday health points, but it is surprising how many would-be champions neglect them in the specialised pursuit of their own particular sport.

Divers, both champions and beginners, should walk as much as possible in their daily routine. Once a week at least, there should be a walk of about six miles, breaking occasionally into a brisk trot of 50 yards or so. The walk should be as relaxed as possible with deep steady breathing.

It is desirable for a diver to join a gymnastic club or have the use of a gymnasium. Agilities such as handsprings, fly-springs and all forms of vaulting are particularly useful.

Weight training as opposed to the actual sport of weight lifting is gaining greater recognition as a necessary adjunct to attaining diving fitness. The method of training implies the use of a carefully worked out series of exercises using weights to overload the various movements. Repetitions of each exercise are performed using a weight which had been found to be within the capacity of the participant's present strength and endurance. There is a gradual increase in the number of repetitions and then a further overload is achieved by reverting to the original number of repetitions with an increased weight. Muscular strength and endurance is quite quickly increased and contrary to former thought, speed of movement is not impaired, indeed it is improved.

Exercises should be carefully selected by an experienced coach for each diver and applied to those muscle groups requiring strengthening. Kept within limits and efficiently supervised, weight training can be extremely beneficial to a diver.

A careful check should be kept on diet. The minimum of starchy foods — potatoes, bread, cakes, etc., is required. Plenty of fresh fruit, milk, salads and meat are the most suitable foods. 'An apple a day' will do a great deal to keep the doctor away.

Anyone doing such a strenuous sport as diving ought to have a periodic medical check-up, once a year at least. This check-up should include a visit to a dentist because bad teeth are perhaps the commonest health fault to be found in athletes — much to their detriment.

Regular habits are most important. The body is a machine which responds well to regularity, particularly of working, eating, emptying the bowels and sleeping. Sleeping is very important. The harder the training the more sleep is required. Ten hours ought to be the minimum amount of sleep for a diver in training.

During training sessions take care to keep warm. If you start shivering, stop work, have a good rub down and get into warm clothing. The greatest danger to English divers is our climate! No one is at his best when cold, and body resistance to all types of disease is reduced. A good supply of towels will help to keep a diver warm during training sessions, and whenever he has to wait between dives, he should stand on a wooden surface if possible — cold stone floors literally drain body-heat away.

Lastly, potential diving champions must realise that the muscle tone of divers and swimmers is fundamentally different. You cannot be a National Champion at both sports. A diver aspiring to the highest levels should restrict his swimming activities to short swims of about 100 yeards. Distance swimming and water polo should be forbidden. Where a diver does 'swim' as well, it should be after a diving session and not before.

CHAPTER X

THE MEDICAL ASPECT OF DIVING

Contributed by **Dr. H. NOEL BLEASDALE, M.B., CH.B.**
(Hon. Medical Adviser to the Amateur Swimming Association)

THE PHYSIOLOGY AND MAINTENANCE OF DIVING EFFORT

Diving is the branch of our sport that appeals to the aspirant for the aesthetic. There is, in sport generally, nothing quite comparable to the art of the diver. It is only to be expected, therefore, that the problems of physiology and pathology, as related to diving, are quite unique.

Physical fitness, the keynote of success in other branches of sport, applies equally to diving. It is recommended that a diver at the commencement of each season undergoes a medical examination, and that certain points are particularly stressed.

The ear, nose and throat should be checked in detail. Chronic middle ear disease is not uncommon amongst divers.

The usual chain of events in this complaint is that infection as from the common cold or septic throat, extends up the Eustachian tube to the middle ear. This may be brought about by direct spread, by faulty blowing of the nose, or by diving when such an infection is present. The middle ear is a small compartment and, as the infection proceeds, pus forms and is under tension. It frequently perforates the drumhead and causes the ear to discharge. When this happens, the infection may subside, and the drum heal, leaving a small scar. On other occasions, as the middle ear is difficult to drain, the discharge becomes chronic, and from time to time pus is discharged from the ear. This clinical picture, so often seen, may be avoided in the first instance by simple common sense precautions, such as avoidance of diving when a victim of septic throats or colds, and by correctly blowing the nose — one nostril at a time. If a diver has an old perforation, medical advice should be sought regarding fitness to compete.

The teeth should be maintained in a good state of repair by regular dental consultations, because they themselves can be the precursors of throat infection.

The diver requires good eyesight if he is to fix accurately on a point in backward take-off dives. He must also be capable of spotting and focussing quickly on the water surface. Hygienic measures are the avoidance of reading or writing in poor light — avoiding exposing the naked eyes to strong sunlight or arc lamps, and the occasional use of a good proprietary eye bath should there be irritation following swimming or diving.

A further point sometimes forgotten by the diver is the care of the feet. If the feet are to acquire the feel of the board and give the maximum take-off, they should be free from afflictions such as corns, bunions, ingrowing toe nails and cracks between the toes, the result of 'athlete's foot'.

One British diver at the London games complained of painful 'take-offs', and X-ray examination revealed rheumatoid arthritis in a joint, complicating an old fracture acquired in 1947.

The physiological principles in diving may be classified in two ways:—

1. Those applicable to any form of exercise, i.e., the effort syndrome.

2. The more delicate faculties of balance which are used in diving in a very specialised way.

The effort syndrome may be seen in diving in an exercise such as bounding the board. On commencing the exercise, the muscles of the limbs contract and propel blood back to the heart more rapidly than at rest, i.e., venous pressure rises.

The increased volume of blood received by the right heart causes it to beat more efficiently, and quicker, and the pulse rate and systemic blood pressure rise to approximately 120/min. and 180 mms. of mercury respectively. At the same time glycogen in the muscles is broken down to carbon dioxide and water, the carbon dioxide being neutralised in the blood stream by alkali and eventually excreted in the lungs.

No great oxygen debt is accumulated in diving, as the effort is only short lived, and in the period between one dive and the next, recovery from the exercise is virtually complete. In the case of the 10-metre board, however, several foot pounds of energy are utilised in climbing the ladders, but in a young diver of good health, the ability to carry out a conversation with a friend on reaching the top stage, is a fair indication of good cardiac and respiratory function.

Balance is achieved by reflexes received by the diver from the outside world.

When he stands on a diving board, his feet tell him that they are on a firm base by means of nerve tracts called the posterior columns, which relay these impulses to conscious levels. The eyes, if he looks at the board, confirm the fact that he is standing on a firm base. If he looks down and his eyes tell him the floor is really 10 metres below him, confusion may occur between the impulses received by the feet and the eyes and dizziness is the result. A diver in training must soon be able to master this confusion or he would never be able to display the confidence seen at the championships. The principle of gaining confidence on the lower boards before the higher ones are attempted appears very sound and this is the method used at an early stage. When the diver has left the board, balance is achieved by two means:

1. Muscle and joint sense, which gives him awareness of the position of the limbs in space relative to the trunk and certain neck righting reflexes which cause the body to follow the head in certain movements.

2. Labyrinthine reflexes which are received by the brain from the circular canals, and which tell the diver whether he is erect, upside down, spinning or twisting

The maintenance of diving effort is the training of the body to develop the physiological principles enumerated above by,

1. Physical fitness.
2. Exercises to improve the heart and circulation, skipping, etc.
3. Exercises to improve grace and rhythm of movement, and to display the limbs to advantage, e.g., ballet.

4. Development of the senses of balance. This may be done on the springboard, trampoline or gymnasium mat.

Even an expert has occasional moments of anxiety. At the London games again, an American diver, a girl, fell heavily during practice. She was not hurt and was sent up again by the coach. It was several minutes before she would straighten out correctly in the air — running header straight — and she seemed to lose control by confusion of the muscle and joint senses and by the psychological fear she would be hurt on landing in the water. Courage is, in my opinion, a very important quality in the diver, and this coupled with understanding of the physiological principles, thorough training and a sense of the aesthetic, will take him far.

THE GIRL DIVER

Physically, the girl diver possesses certain advantages over her male counterpart.

She is usually smaller, her bones are lighter, her muscles less bulky, and she frequently possesses more mobility due to laxity of her ligaments. These features tend to make her movements in diving more graceful than the male, and as she is often more emotional, if emotion is controlled, she can utilise it in her diving to produce what we usually term the 'poetry of motion'.

She does possess, at certain periods, distinct disadvantages which may cause her to vary in consistency more than is the case in the male competitor.

Her reactions to menstruation are variable. Some girls are hardly troubled at all. Others, for a day or two, feel listless, and the body temperature is frequently raised to that of the actual flow, there may be a dull rhythmical backache, radiating to the limbs which feel heavy. There is often tenderness in the breasts. Emotionally, the girl may be easily upset by chance remarks, and in competition may take it badly if she does not succeed. A girl who feels so ill that she is unable to continue with school or office work at these times should seek medical advice.

The question of training under these conditions might be left to her parents who, of course, know her best, but if the girl herself feels quite well, and has no abdominal tenderness, diving should not do her any harm provided that she is adequately protected. A good indication is to ask the girl whether she undertook gymnastics and school games during her 'periods' and, if so, it gives the information as to her usual degree of disability.

If a girl is taken ill on a course, the first essentials are bed, warmth and hot drinks. Aspirin gr. 10 three times during the day is valuable, but if the symptoms do not subside rapidly under these conditions, a doctor should be consulted, for only a medical man can correlate the nature of her symptoms with her previous medical history. There is no evidence to suggest that a girl who has taken part in diving — or sport generally, suffers from any handicap later in life during childbirth, in fact, what evidence we have before us is to the contrary.

APPENDIX

1. A.S.A. CHAMPIONSHIP CONDITIONS

Full details of these conditions are published in the A.S.A. Handbook. It should be noted that the water depths and areas required for A.S.A. Diving Championships are the same as those laid down by the F.I.N.A.

2. A.S.A. EXAMINATIONS FOR TEACHERS CERTIFICATE FOR DIVING AND DIVING COACHES CERTIFICATE

Details of the following examinations, including Application Forms, can be obtained from the A.S.A. Hon. Secretary, 64 Cannon Street, London, E.C.4.

A.S.A. Teachers Certificate for Diving.

A.S.A. Coaches Certificate for Diving.

3. PROFICIENCY TESTS

The aim of these Tests is to raise the standard of diving throughout the country. Combined Application and Judging Forms, covering the Bronze, Silver and Gold Standards, can be obtained from the Organiser, Miss L. V. Cook, 12 Kings Avenue, Woodford Green, Essex. Telephone: BUCkhurst 9361.

THE TESTS

Dives of the same number shall count as the same dive.

Bronze Standard. Ladies and Men. Five voluntary dives from a 1 or 3 metre springboard, selected from at least three different groups. The whole test must be performed from the same board height.

Silver Standard, Springboard—
Ladies: ⎱ 6 voluntary dives from a 1 or 3 metre spring-
Men: ⎰ board, selected from five different groups.
The whole test must be performed from the same board height.

Silver Standard, High Board—
Ladies: 5 voluntary dives from a 5 metre board, selected from at least 4 different groups.
Men: 6 voluntary dives from a 5 metre board, selected from at least 5 different groups.

Gold Standard, Springboard—

Ladies: } 10 voluntary dives from 3 metre springboard,
Men: } 2 dives to be selected from each group.

Gold Standard, High Board—

Ladies: 3 voluntary dives from 10 metres, and 3 voluntary dives from 5 or 10 metres, selected from at least 4 different groups.

Men: 8 voluntary dives from 10 metres, 5 of which must be selected each from a differerent group.

An applicant shall make his own arrangements to take the test which must be judged as follows:—

Bronze: Two diving judges on the official list of any County or District Association.

Silver: Two diving judges on the official list of any District Association.

Gold: Three diving judges, two of whom must be from the official list of the A.S.A. The third judge may be selected from the Subsidiary List.

In judging these tests, tariff values shall not be taken into consideration. The judges' awards shall be aggregated, and the following percentages shall be required to obtain a pass:—

Bronze—45 per cent; Silver—50 per cent.; Gold—55 per cent.

The diving tables of the Federation Internationale de Natation Amateur shall be used in connection with these tests.

Successful candidates shall be awarded a badge, either buttonhole or brooch type, appropriate to the test passed, and be entitled to purchase a costume badge of similar design at a cost of 5/- Replacement badges of either type may be purchased price, 5/-.

Applications for the Silver Standard award shall be accepted only from holders of the Bronze Standard, and applications for the Gold Standard award shall be accepted only from holders of the Silver Standard.

Applications must be made on the official forms, and accompanied by a registration fee of six shillings.

Details of the awards obtained shall be recorded in a National Divers' Register, and applications may, if desired, be made for both Springboard and High board, in any one standard.

4. A.S.A. PUBLICATIONS, FILMS AND LOOPS

The Association publishes a wide range of books covering all aspects of the sport and possesses a number of films and film loops, in black/white and colour dealing with both swimming and diving. Films and loops in both 16 mm. and 8 mm. are available for purchase and/or hire. Full details are given in a separate leaflet obtainable from the Hon. Secretary, A.S.A. 64 Cannon Street, London, E.C.4.

5. DIVING REQUISITES

Applications for the following Diving Requisites should be sent together with remittance, to Miss L. V. Cook, 12 Kings Avenue, Woodford Green, Essex. Telephone: BUCkhurst 9361.

Judging Numbers	6/8 per pack
Plain Diving Judging Sheets	2/- per doz.
Recording Sheets (Fancy Diving)	3/- per doz.
Championship Recording Sheets	25/- per pad
(in triplicate)	(50 sets)